CW01394612

Women of P(
The Woman As Magus

Jaq D Hawkins

www.capallbann.co.uk

Women of Power
The Woman As Magus

©Copyright Jaq D Hawkins 2006

ISBN 186163 241 X

ALL RIGHTS RESERVED

No part of this publication may be reproduced, stored in a retrieval system or transmitted in any form or by any means, electronic, mechanical, photocopying, scanning, recording or otherwise without the prior written permission of the author and the publisher.

Cover design by HR Design

Published by:

Capall Bann Publishing
Auton Farm
Milverton
Somerset
TA4 1NE

In memory of my mother,

My first teacher in the magic

of the Feminine Arts

Beverly Hawley
1929-2006

Other titles by Jaq D Hawkins, also published by Capall Bann:

Understanding Chaos Magic
Chaos Monkey
Spirits of the Earth
Spirits of the Air
Spirits of the Fire
Spirits of the Water
Spirits of the Aether

Contents

"No fair! I never get quoted! I want a reference as someone who inspired you!"

- Diablo Verde

Yeah, but there are lots of people like me out there, people with ethics... Dangerous people.

- Diablo Verde

Chapter One

A Woman's Place in Magic

Gender has been the subject of many conversations about magic over many years. One hears of 'women's intuition', yet there was a time when women were not allowed to practice magic in more than one culture. Some historians claim precedent for matriarchal societies where women held power both politically and magically. There are many arguments both for and against the evidence for these histories, and there is little doubt that the suppression of women in very patriarchal societies is based in fear of the effects that a woman may have over a man, certainly sexually. If we look into the subject deeply enough, we may find that fear of women is also based in the effects that they instinctively accomplish magically.

Since the 1960's, there has been an explosion of material made available for students of the occult and new age. Some texts from the 1800's have been reprinted in easily available paperback form. Others which are older, particularly books on medieval alchemy, are perhaps less easily available but can be obtained in reprint forms. The authors of the various old books of magic are almost exclusively men, with the exception of Helena Petrovna Blavatsky (1831-1891). Starting in the 1960's, a surge of women authors appear, primarily producing books on witchcraft and new age philosophy, followed by the self-help book phenomenon. However, most of the books on ceremonial magic continue to be written by men, despite significant numbers of female members existing in ceremonial magical Orders. The exceptions can be counted on one hand; most notable is Nema, the author of *Maat Magick* (York Beach, ME: Samuel Weiser, 1995) which has become required reading among magicians of many paths. There are a few others, but mostly the texts seem to balance between Wicca and Magic(k) and perpetuate the impression that witchcraft is a woman's realm, while Magic(k) is primarily associated with the masculine.

I find this state of affairs curious, because I have met other woman magicians besides myself who have a similar approach to ceremonial or even chaos magic. Many of these claimed to be 'writing a book', a perpetual state which in many people never actually leads to producing a finished manuscript. This is common to both men and women, yet the imbalance of authors of books which appear on the shelves of bookstores continues. Women can hardly blame men for this, as many of the editors of 'new age' publications are women and female authors continue to produce books on witchcraft and related subjects in abundance. I personally did not encounter any form of gender prejudice in my attempts to get my first book on chaos magic published. In fact, three publishers were interested. Yet there are no other books on chaos magic by female authors widely published at the time of this writing, seven years after my first book was originally published.

This would not seem so odd if there were few women who practice chaos magic or who write, but this is not the case. Perhaps I have not come across an equal number of female chaos magicians to male, but there is certainly no lack of them and many of them are very serious magicians whom I respect. Two of those I know are currently 'writing a book'.

Exceptions can be found to these generalisations of course, and as time goes on more books on witchcraft and paganism in general are appearing by male authors although still just a few women have delved into the ceremonial magic area of published work. Even some of those have mixed the disciplines of ceremonial magic into a largely pagan/witch-craft structure. This can partly be explained by the availability of books on magic in general. The most accessible tend to lean toward Wicca, while those on areas of magic such as Alchemy, Hermeticism and Cabbalah are often less available, tend toward dry, intellectual reading, and are often couched in a religious structure that puts off the devoted pagan reader.

Most of the old magic books on subjects like Alchemy were written by men who had legitimate concerns that they could be accused of Christian heresy if they did not couch their writings in Christian symbolism. In fact, many of them were practising Christians, and believed that the power of magic came from the Christian God. This is reflected in the interpretations of magical phenomena, such as in the writings of Dr. John Dee who was astrologer to Queen Elisabeth I. John Dee is best known for attributing much of magic to the power of a hierarchy of Angels. This belief system carried on even with magicians such as Aleister Crowley, who was named the Great Beast by his own parents for his blasphemies to their religion. The symbolism of Christianity carries on in his interpretation of a personal spirit as his 'Holy Guardian Angel'. I have read one fairly well known twentieth century male author who actually states that this sort of magic is 'the only true magic'. As limiting as this viewpoint may be, it illustrates the separatist and elitist attitude which has accompanied the study of ceremonial magic, also called 'High Magic' in reflection of this attitude, through the centuries through which it has developed.

Historically, women before the twentieth century have had less access to magical knowledge than men in general. There are exceptions to this of course. In Ancient Egypt, a culture which focused much attention on magic, women who became priestesses or held high positions in society were directly involved in magic, mostly in the form of serving the gods and goddesses of Egypt. This didn't greatly affect the peasant classes who had no leisure for such activities. Unlike today's churches and Temples, the Temples of Egypt were not frequented by common people, but were maintained by those who dedicated their lives to the purpose of serving various deities.

The actual legal status of women in Egypt was one of equality and they often became traders or practised businesses of various sorts. More of a woman's freedom to live as she pleased was determined by class than by her gender. However, women were not known to hold public offices such as scribes. A Royal Wife was respected in matters of govern-ment and would indeed rule the country if the Pharaoh were away on business or at war, and there were actually four instances of women who actually held the position of Pharaoh. In some ways, the life of a woman in Egypt was not really so different from the life of women in Medieval England, where women of the peasant classes were treated as property and expected to maintain her place as a domestic labourer, while those of the tradesman classes might run their husband's business while he was away or after his death. The actual legal status of these women was not one of equality as in Egypt, but in practice their sphere of influence was similar. The wives of the gentry could be influential through their husbands, if not officially, and the Queen held genuine power of her own although she could be superseded by her husband. In the later middle ages, when King Henry VI was known to lose his reason, his wife, Queen Margaret, actually ran the country for four years from 1456 – 1460.

Magic up to this point in history was largely the preserve of priestly classes, which were usually comprised of men with the notable exception of Ancient Egypt. However, Egypt's legacy of alchemic magic was the exception to this and could be studied away from the preserves of religions. We don't often hear of the women alchemists through history, despite some of the most important contributions made by them even in the earliest days. It is only late in the nineteenth century that women magicians begin to become apparent in printed works. While Dr John Dee (1527-1608) was known to practice with a male assistant, by the late nineteenth century magicians such as Aleister Crowley and Austin Spare are known to actively practise magic with women and their journals (*The Equinox* edited by Crowley, *Form and The Golden Hind* edited by Spare) publish articles by women authors whom they obviously respected. Madame Blavatsky (1831-1891) formed the Theosophical Society during this magical era, and the first official initiate to the original Golden Dawn, a well known Magical Order, was one of four women who were among the founding members.

Another century later, women are active in most known Magical Orders. Chaos Magic Orders are also well populated by women members. Still, although articles appear by other women in magazines such as Chaos International, my books on Chaos Magic stand among the well known male authors on the bookshelf representing the female aspects of chaos in solitude. One wonders why this should be, when modern women are writing books on the various aspects of Paganism in plenty.

To understand this odd division requires a look into the history of magic, especially into the area of Alchemy where we find some of the most important lessons of the nature of magic and how it works within the parameters of the balance of the physical and spiritual world in which we exist. We also must look at the effects of the social conditions that have shaped history, and the essential lessons of magic which have been missed in translation over the centuries. In the many conversations I've shared with other magicians about the older texts of magic which can still be obtained in some form, it has been accepted as common knowledge that somewhere along the way, some things have been deliberately hidden or changed in the texts. More significantly, some of us have been aware that not all of the changes have been intentional, and that some essential information has been lost.

In the next chapter, the progression of alchemy is examined in such a way that the omissions become blindingly obvious. Much of what has been lost in the records of ancient magic concerns the feminine principle, working in harmony with the masculine principle. This is something which has survived in Taoism and Taoist alchemy which teaches balance in all things, but has been filtered out of alchemy during its journey through cultures which follow monotheist beliefs. Ironically, this journey started with a woman who contributed significantly to the history and practice of alchemy, Maria the Jewess.

Masculine and feminine balance is not to be confused with polarity, as any system of duality is subject to imbalance. The concepts of yin and yang in Chinese philosophy describe the principles as active (yang, male) and receptive (yin, female). Both aspects must work in perfect harmony to achieve spiritual perfection which is the goal of spiritual alchemy. The physical manifestation which is demonstrated through the transmutation of metals was lost completely to many of the best known European Alchemists, including Paracelsus.

Again, we have two balancing principles, the physical and the spiritual, which must work in harmony to achieve the desired magic. The few European alchemists who were reported to have achieved success in physical alchemy were usually known to work in co-operation with a woman. The others, those who failed, left a legacy of incomplete magic, which would eventually filter down to us as the modern New Age of magic.

It is no wonder that modern pagan women seldom relate to the area of magic which has resulted from centuries of monotheistic and patriarchal dilution. The establishment of nineteenth century magical Orders opened up opportunities for women to practice ceremonial magic(k) in conjunction with male magicians, many of whom respected the women among their groups as serious magicians. However, the social climate of Western culture at the time was steeped in Christian morality. Celibacy was considered a virtue, even between married couples in some cases, and freedom of expression was inhibited in ritual except in the most secretive of circumstances where 'getting caught' in the act of breaking social taboos was a constant fear, and an ever-present limitation.

This state of affairs was seriously challenged by the escapades of Aleister Crowley. Openly defying convention, Crowley attempted to revive magic by seeking the knowledge from its Egyptian roots. However, through drug addiction and a penchant for attracting attention through outrageous behaviour, his accomplishments were partially obscured by a negative public perception that would cause a schism in the magical community for generations to come. He brought the feminine principle back into magical practice through his concept of the Scarlet Woman and the Magical Child, only to be dismissed as a letch by a large portion of the women who would seek a magical path. However, after the dust of the sexual revolution of the 1960's was settled, public perception had changed sufficiently that women began to take an interest in the knowledge, without rejecting the possibility that sex may play a part in legitimate magical practice.

Even by 1954 when Gerald Gardner was creating the tradition which would become modern Wicca, women who were drawn to magic were beginning to push the boundaries of social tradition and to examine for themselves what magic had to offer to them beyond the roles which society had cast for them. The social upheavals of the hippy era and the feminist movement a decade later would open the question for many women of what role she wished to play in her life. Some tried perhaps a bit too hard to prove they were the same as men in the workforce, sometimes even denying the qualities which make us women. Some slipped easily into the nurturing roles of the Earth Mother, which is easily compatible with the growth of Wicca and by the 1980's had taken to extensive networking through small magazines and the growing phenomenon of the internet.

Now, as the twenty-first century is gaining momentum, women have a plethora of choices within the magical community. Social changes have affected the old Orders so that they are not always the stuffy institutions that once existed, and Chaos Magic has opened up a realm of independent methods over the quarter of a century in that it has existed as such. Even the Wicca and witchcraft paths have diverged into many trajectories of practice which range from very 'by-the-book' traditions to the totally eclectic road. The crossover from one path of magic to another has become smoother than at any other time of history. Wicca and witchcraft have become identifiable primarily through the religious overtones of goddess worship, while the path of the magician continues to be one of study of magic itself, with less emphasis on the Judeo-Christian beliefs that overshadowed its practices for several centuries.

A woman can now choose freely among the paths of magic that are available. Materials for study are commercially obtainable so much that there is more of a challenge in weeding through the dross for the real gems of wisdom than in finding information on magic as was once the case. Some ceremonial Orders actually seek to increase their female membership. Women are particularly respected in the goddess oriented religions, and this may be why so many women are drawn to them, apart from the continued networking which has made Wicca the public face of magic in the Western world.

But still, there are a number of women who choose the path of the magician. Some spend some time in the Orders, while many others practice quietly either on their own, or with a friend or two whom they trust. Some of us meet each other in passing on occasion, and recognise that quality which makes us 'different' even among the magical community. The deeper study of magic is a calling that cannot be satisfied with reading a few modern books or with rituals of seasonal celebration. The women who seek an understanding of their power as woman as well as of the ancient magical practices which are referenced in the newer books have much knowledge available to them in this age, and those who have eyes to see may learn that there is a special power in being simply what they are: Women Magicians.

"Egypt was the Mother of Magicians"
                                           - Clement of Alexandria

"That's so last Aeon darling."
                                           - Diablo Verde

Chapter Two

Ancient Teachings and Texts of Wisdom

Many of today's magicians seek wisdom in ancient texts. Some of the better known volumes have been reprinted, others have been extensively quoted in modern books on magic. Still the quest goes on, much of it through antique book sellers and the internet, for knowledge from the past that may be applied to the magic of the present.

Much of the focus on these tomes of wisdom focuses on the Medieval books of Alchemy. Some scholars have moved beyond the reprinted texts to study the wealth of information which may be found in Egyptian Hermeticism, yet many remain ignorant of the diversity of cultures which have discovered the secrets of Alchemy, and the place that women Alchemists have filled within these cultures.

In China, Alchemy is dated 200 years before Christ and is directly associated with Taoism. The saying goes that all Alchemists are Taoists, but not all Taoists are Alchemists.

Chinese Alchemists also tend to be doctors. The procedures for turning base metals into gold are much the same as the better known Medieval English Alchemists, but the focus is more on longevity and immortality than on the material aspects of gold making. Gold is used as an elixir, generally created from mercury and arsenic, and some ingredients which are less clear. The intent is that it should be ingested in order to achieve immortality. Too often, ingesting the poisons which are used in the process has lead instead to death.

The Philosopher's Stone is referred to in China as the Pill of Immortality. It is thought among the Chinese Alchemists that such a pill can be created in the alembic from cinnabar, which is thought to be mercuric sulphide. This is part of the *Wai Tan*, or outer elixir of Alchemy. The *Nei Tan*, the inner elixir, manifests through Qigong, a method of breath control, and Tai Chi, a practice of martial arts exercise which develops suppleness of the body. Many also practice purification through diet.

Alchemy is the art and science of transformation, and the intent of the *Nei Tan* is to transform and renew the body through these practices. Taoism is a religion of immortality and the ways in which to achieve the perfect state which will allow the body to continue indefinitely. Sexual magic practices are included in techniques to preserve the spiritual energy, called *Chi*. Many have heard of these techniques among modern magicians, and especially of the technique whereby the male retains ejaculation during orgasm. However, women are also active participants in the practices of Taoist sexual magic.

Women often held prominent positions in alchemical circles in China. There is a story about the alchemist Cheng Wei who was unsuccessful when trying to make gold following the directions of the *Chen Chung Hung Pao* book, until his wife who came from a family of skilled adepts in the magical arts assisted him by throwing an unknown substance into the vessel, which turned the mixture into silver. She had in fact studied under one of the Emperor Wu Ti's favourite concubines, who had been an expert in Taoist sexual techniques for prolonging life. It would seem that the *Wai Tan* and the *Nei Tan* work in harmony, as the inner and outer mysteries of Alchemy in every culture must do.

Much of the philosophy of Taoism is associated with a receptive attitude, which is considered the 'feminine' approach to life. In Chinese, 'woman' is literally translated as the 'Mysterious Feminine.' Living creatures are believed to be surrounded by *yin*, the feminine, and to envelop *yang*, the masculine. At the basis of Taoist cosmology is the Chi, which circulates around the body as well as the universe and might be compared to *the force* popularised in the Star Wars films. It is the life force which pervades all and is responsible for regeneration and growth, as well as for maintaining the structure of the physical.

The Tao divides into the balance of yin and yang, which ebb and flow like waves in the ocean, maintaining the naturally chaotic balance of all that exists. Beyond that, all divides into the five elements; water, fire, wood, metal and earth. These elements correspond to the five visible planets, and are considered active forces and sorts of processes rather than constituents as in the Western idea of the elements.

The Taoists believe that we all have the power to decide our own life span, and that it is only worldly conditioning which leads to decay and death through our own expectations of the ravages of time. Many of us have observed an acquaintance or family member suddenly 'get old' after the loss of a loved one or a life tragedy, or even the passing of a significant birthday or other event. The philosophy of the Taoists, while contrary to what many of us accept as scientific logic, embraces the core of the mysteries of Alchemy, the art and science of transmutation. The wisdom of the Tao can allow a change in belief and manifestation of the principles of ageing more sensibly than the bottled concoctions that women spend large amounts of money to obtain, in the belief that the next cream or treatment may delay the visible signs of age. Far more effective are the practices which maintain the breath, the physical suppleness, the sexual *chi*, and regenerative qualities of the attitude of positive acceptance of life and joy in simple pleasures.

Life energy manipulation is similarly practised in Indian Alchemy, and in fact many of the life preserving practices as well as the outer Alchemy methods of transmutations are so similar between India and China that it is likely that they have developed from common roots. Most notable is the balance of male and female in the medical practice of Ayurveda, which is closely linked to Indian Alchemy. This also relates closely to Tantra, where the practices of ritual sex have become well known. Author Peter Marshall (*The Philosopher's Stone: A Quest for the Secrets of Alchemy*. London: Pan Books, 2001) postulates that women in India once held a position of equality in the practice of Tantric Alchemy, based on the explicit carvings which were found on ancient temples in 1838 by T. S. Burt, a British engineer. However, in his book, there are no references to female Alchemists as there are in China. Both cultures are male dominated throughout recorded history. Both show evidence that the women played an active role in sexual magical practices, yet between the two of them, only China records incidences of women who practice the magical arts independently of their husbands.

Indian Alchemy is referred to as the 'handmaid of medicine'. As in China, it is usually practised by doctors. The mixture of religions in India results in some differences in cultural approach to Alchemy, but there are very close similarities, especially in Tantra, to Taoist Alchemy. In Tantra, the feminine aspect of nature is the principle of acceptance, rather than negation. The Tantrist learns to maintain a sense of identity during passion, and to avoid losing himself within ecstasy. Female orgasm is encouraged, as it moves energy around but like the Taoists, the male attempts to preserve the seminal fluids.

It is in India that we first find the proverb, "When the pupil is ready, the Guru will appear". Variations of this adage permeate many philosophies of modern magic. It is also from India that we get the concept of *Kundalini*, the female serpent that takes form at the perineum and rises through the spinal chord, waking cosmic energy as it passes through the chakras to the crown of the head. The process is meant to purify, just as the Indian Alchemists believe that they are able to purify the polluted waters of the Ganga river, and to enable one to free himself from the empirical world and to reach the kingdom of heaven. It is a transformative process, intended to bring enlightenment.

Indian Alchemy is thought to be imperfect by the Tibetan Alchemists who live in India. The process of purifying mercury to remove its poisonous qualities is far longer and more elaborate in Tibetan Alchemy, taking two months to create their own version of the pill of immortality. It is also believed by them that the pill is unnecessary for those who reach perfection through the inner Alchemy, achieved through exercise, diet and meditation. In all of the Eastern philosophies, making gold is seen as a means to an end in the spiritual realm, with little emphasis on the materialist aspects of outer Alchemy.

Alchemy, of course, originates in Egypt. The Arab word *Al-Kemia* literally means the 'Black Land', and refers to Egypt. The arts of preservation that Egypt are so well known for are Alchemic Arts, although in Egypt itself they were named for the god Hermes after the Greek occupation in 332 B C.

Hermes was considered to be the equivalent of the Egyptian god Thoth, who is thought of as the father of Alchemy. There is some speculation that one of the substances used in the art of mummification, known as red mercury, may well be the philosopher's stone.

Unlike many historic conquerors, the Greeks embraced the culture of Egypt, but added their own influence to Egyptian Alchemy. It was the Greeks who introduced the concept of the four elements, Earth, Air, Fire and Water, as the constituents of all matter. Aristotle had added Aether as the fifth element of Spirit, which in description compares with the Egyptian *heka*, their word for magic. The Egyptian concept of magic is as one of the forces of the god Atum, the power to create order out of the primeval chaos. It is represented by what many have thought to be an eye (actually the haunch of a lion, a symbol for power) which is the hieroglyph for 'to create'. All acts of magic are considered to be part of the continuing creative process.

The Greeks also reversed the polarities of the earth and sky, which to the Egyptian were represented by the female principle in the sky (Isis) and the male principle on the earth. The Egyptians recognised the feminine principle of intuition as an important aspect of magic.

Women in Egypt had always enjoyed official equality in status to men of their own class, and even in Greek occupied Egypt women alchemists played an important role in the development of the Art. Most notable were Cleopatra (not the well-known Pharaoh Cleopatra who was Cleopatra VII), Maria the Jewess, and Theosebia, who worked closely with Zosimus such that he dedicated his twenty-eight books titled *Alchemical Matters* to her.

Peter Marshall tells us that Cleopatra was noted to write in a "poetic and exuberant way which is rare among the early alchemists." Her intuitive understanding of the link between the transformation of metals and the purification of the soul was appreciated and developed by later alchemists. She used sexual imagery to relate the alchemical process to the harmony of nature, a concept which has become a key feature to the understanding of Alchemy.

Maria attached religious significance to the Art, as she came from the Jewish tradition. She believed that lustful angels brought the arts of metallurgy and dyeing to mankind and begat children on the 'daughters of men'. She approached the art of purification from a religious perspective, but as a result of her experiments she perfected the distillation of liquids and invented the bain-marie, which is still used in kitchens and laboratories world-wide. She also invented the tribikos, which is a still with three funnels and receivers where the distilled vapours are condensed, and the kerotakis, which is a reflux apparatus for treating metals with vapours for colouration. These instruments have changed little over the history of Alchemy since Maria's time, and their significance to alchemical study is considerable.

Zosimus, whose name is synonymous with fourth century Alchemy, sought his wisdom from the Egyptian temples. This may be where he met Theosebia, who was a priestess who attracted a secret circle of initiates. By this time, the need for secrecy among the alchemists was becoming apparent, as the Romans sought to eradicate the Art from Egypt. His writings were coloured by the fantastic imagery he found in vivid dreams, which provided a significant amount of allegory for the spiritual aspects of Alchemy. He regarded Theosebia as a 'sister' in the Art, and urged her to calm her passions and follow a religious path, rather than the path of Aristotle which he saw as a 'visible and mortal' path. He emphasised Spiritual Alchemy, and regarded gold as spirit apart from the substance.

There is some evidence to suggest that all of the ancient civilisations may have a common root from a lost civilisation, possibly the Atlantis that Plato spoke of. Many of Egypt's monuments have hieroglyphic writing carved into their internal walls which tell of the Ancient Egyptian beliefs and histories. These have provided a wealth of information about Egypt for archaeologists since they first learned to translate the hieroglyphs after the discovery of the Rosetta Stone. On the walls of Dendara Temple, 50 kilometres north of Luxor, an inscription in one of the subterranean crypts states that the Temple was built 'according to a plan written in ancient writing upon a goat skin scroll from the time of the Companions of Horus'. This is a reference to a race of exceptional beings who ruled Egypt during the 'First Time', a reference which is believed to allude to a people who came from across the sea from a lost civilisation after a flood, bringing the arts of Alchemy with them as well as other wonders.

Dendara was built on an earlier site in the first century B C, and is dedicated to Hathor, the goddess of love and fertility. It was once a site of pilgrimage where alchemical elixirs and magical therapies were performed. Hathor is considered a patroness of healing, and is the daughter of Re. She was called 'The Golden One', and mirrors made of gold were decorated with her image or symbol. Dendara has various Alchemical formulae on the walls of other chambers, and contained the only circular zodiac found in Egypt which is now at the Louvre museum in Paris.

The connection between Alchemy and astrology is prevalent in India, but in Egypt they go hand in hand. In Egypt, however, rather than a dualistic concept of male and female they believed that there were nine different aspects of the self.

According to Dr. Kwabena F. Ashanti is his *Rootwork and Voodoo in Mental Health*, (Durham, NC: Tone Books,1987) these parts are:

(1) The Ka -the abstract personality of the individual to whom it belongs, Possessing the form and attributes of a human with power of movement omnipresence, and ability to receive nourishment. Equivalent to what we call the shadow image.

(2) The Khat - the mortal concrete personality, the physical body.

(3) The Ba- the heart-soul, which lives in the Ka and sometimes beside it, to supply the Ka with food and air. Capable of metamorphosis.

(4) The Ab- the heart, the physical life in humans, spiritual, rational and ethical. Associated with the Ba(heart-soul). In the Egyptian Judgement Drama, it undergoes examination in the presence of the God Osiers, the great creator and judge of the dead.

(5) The Kaibit-the shadow. Also associated with the Ba, from which it receives its nourishments. Has the power of movement and omnipresence.

(6) The Khu-spiritual soul that lives forever. A heavenly being, closely associated with the Ba.

(7) The Sahu- the spiritual body in which the Khu or spiritual soul dwells. The moral nature of mental and spiritual qualities is united to form new powers that man has the choice to use for good or evil.

(8) The Sekhem- the power or spirit of the vital force in humans. Lives in the heavens with the spirit of Khu.

(9) The Ren- the name of an individual, the essential attribute for preservation of a being. The ancients believed that in the absence of a name, the individual ceased to exist. The quality of a name, therefore, was very important.

According to Ashanti, there were nine original gods in the religion of the Ancient Egyptians. They were:

(1) Shu, the God of air;

(2) Tefnut, the Goddess of Moisture;

(3) Geb, the God of Earth; and

(4) Nut, Goddess of the sky; universe

These Gods gave birth to

(5) Osiris, the God of omnipotence and omniscience;

(6) Isis, the wife of Osiris, the female principle;

(7) Seth, the God of evil, opposite good;

(8) Nephthys, wife of Seth, and

(9) Atum(Atom), the creator God of Gods.

Many of Egypt's secrets are yet undiscovered. The Sphinx, which is dated thousands of years earlier than the pyramids, has never been thoroughly explored. There has been much speculation about what treasures of knowledge may lie within a 12 by 15 meter chamber which lies between its paws, yet any attempts to investigate have met with resistance of one kind or another and the secrets continue to lie hidden.

In the seventh century, Egypt was conquered again, this time by the Muslims who became the heirs to Egyptian alchemy. The monotheism which Maria the Jewess had imposed on the alchemical philosophy would be further adapted to the religion of Islam, and its believers would bring Alchemy to Europe in the next century when the Moors invaded southern Spain. It was a woman, a Visigoth sorceress, who would undo Islamic rule in Spain, and the Christians would yet again paint a picture of Alchemy that would attribute its marvellous powers to their own God. The Visigoths Had been increasingly Christianised since the fourth century, so that by the eighth century their Arian roots had been effectively forgotten. Alchemy would have to wait a few more centuries to fall back into the hands of academics and magicians who would recognise the importance of Ancient Egyptian philosophy in its most basic tenets.

The Muslims contributed much to alchemic literature, including the Picatrix, a translation of The Emerald Tablet, and the concept of magic squares. In 750, Baghdad was the centre of learning for magicians and alchemists. They believed Hermes to be the father of Alchemy and developed much of the philosophy that is found in modern books on the subject. The melding of Cabalistic philosophy with the Hermetic tradition was also occurring between the sixth and tenth centuries so that by the time the Zohar was written around c1275, the imposition of monotheistic religion had become an integral part of alchemical literature that would influence students of magic even up to the present.

The development of Outer Alchemy saw so much progress from the Arabic culture that many of the words we still use today have their roots in the Arabic language. Over 500 years the Muslims made great strides in the art of refinement of materials, including discovering the technique of making clear glass from sand which was first perfected in Córdoba. It is perhaps ironic than an art which emphasises removing impurities to achieve perfection had wandered so far from the origins of the art of inner, or Spiritual Alchemy. The texts on Alchemy continually stress the importance of the spiritual aspect of the Art and the balance between the masculine and feminine principles, what the Chinese would term the yin and yang. This aspect continued to be featured in the Muslim and European texts, but had been committed to allegory repeatedly since Maria had first used this method to reconcile her Art with her religion, so much so that the attribution of all the spiritual power of the alchemical art was now attributed to the God of the Jews, Christians or Muslims. As a result of the imposition of monotheistic religion, the Art had lost its connections to magic. The result of this was of course many failed experiments, as the later alchemists attempted to produce physical results of Outer Alchemy with only allegory and superstition to guide them through the spiritual aspects. Many of the alchemists of the Islamic and Christian cultures would repeat the same research and experiments over and over again, reinventing Alchemy continually and developing many important scientific discoveries in the process of looking for the elusive secret to transmutation which lay hidden within the adulterated texts.

The Chinese had developed their own tradition of Alchemy separately from the Islamic legacy and had little effect on the study in Europe. While the Europeans like St Aquinas who wrote extensively about the female apparition of God as Sophia, the Gnostic Goddess of Wisdom, in order to seek the balance of the male and female principles in Alchemy, the Chinese found a natural balance in the Taoist philosophy and, although they had little contact with the West, more recent contacts with the Chinese alchemists would indicate that they have had much more success in the quest for immortality which lies at the heart of Spiritual Alchemy. Some of this tradition appears to have found its way to the Sufi philosophy as well. The Sufi's are well known for achieving marvels through meditation techniques and various forms of magic.

The Arabic texts are of great value to modern alchemists, so long as one remembers to 'read between the lines'. Their achievements in the physical realm of transmutation of substances are unequalled since the time of the Egyptians, and much of the spiritual aspects still lie hidden within the allegory and devotion to a monotheistic God who was non-existent to the Ancient Egyptians. The ascetic religious approach may not have affected the application of outer alchemy were it not for the intermarriage of the inner and outer traditions, and the necessity of finding the spiritual secrets to purification in order to correctly perform the transmutation of metals. The later Christian alchemists would interpret the need for purification within the context of their own morality, leaving their alchemical experiments sexless and unproductive. Official church objection to the magical arts led to the Romans burning alchemical books in 292 AD and to a papal bull from Pope John XXII in 1317 forbidding the practice of Alchemy. Despite this, church officials took a great deal of interest in the potential material benefits of making gold and would support the efforts of alchemists secretly. The occasional monk would practice the Art behind the protective walls of a monastery, and a few wealthy citizens were able to carry out their own experiments quietly.

There were far more charlatans and failed experiments than successes. The emphasis on the physical transmutation of metals was only half of the Art. The most successful alchemists in history were those who regarded the physical transmutation as a manifestation of spiritual transformation, in particular within those cultures where Sexual Alchemy was freely practised. There were however, a few known successes among the European alchemists. Thomas Norton (1433-1513), who came from a renowned Bristol family, claimed to have achieved the successful preparation of the Great Red Elixir, but that it had been stolen by a servant. Nothing is reported about what may have happened to this elixir. Norton tried again, and again claimed that he was successful, but that this time it was stolen by a woman, perhaps the wife of William Canynges who was said to have rebuilt the Church of St Mary Redcliffe with money made from the elixir.

Norton insisted that most of the books of recipes for the elixir were 'deceits', and that an alchemist must understand the how and why of alchemical operations. Those who approach Alchemy with the goal of attaining riches were doomed to failure. The studies of Alchemy and Caballa gave rise to esoteric symbolism in many of the medieval cathedrals. In France the most notable of these are Chartres and Notre Dame, which is in Paris not far from the home of the most well known successful European alchemist, Nicolas Flamel.

No explanation for the wealth of Flamel has ever been determined, and rumours of his successful experiments as well as sightings of himself and his wife long after they were reported to be dead have given rise to speculation and even legends of his successful alchemical operations. He recorded a successful transmutation in 1382. Interestingly, one of the unique qualities of Flamel's work is that he was closely assisted by his wife, Perennelle, whom he said, '...understood it as well as I, because she helped me in my operations, and without doubt if she had undertaken to do it herself she would have attained to the end and perfection thereof.'

Legends of immortality have followed the reputations of a few of the later alchemists, among them St Germain in the 18th century and Fulcanelli in the 20th century. Whether the rumours are true or as apocryphal as sightings of Elvis and Bruce Lee is undeterminable. However, we do know that one of the best known and greatest contributors to European philosophical alchemy, Paracelsus, died in poverty at the age of 48. Paracelsus had a confrontational disposition which undoubtedly alienated his contemporaries and led to his downfall, yet conversely it was his writings on the philosophical aspects of Alchemy which have become some of the most important of the European texts of history. He reintroduced salt as the third element in harmony with the alchemic sulphur and mercury to form a triad of body, soul and spirit. Many today would re-interpret this as body, mind and spirit.

Despite his temperament, he attracted followers through pure genius and a spiritual vision which had been lacking in the search for gold among many of the European alchemists. It was from the ranks of his followers after his death that a new magical Order, the Fraternity of the Rosy Cross, would form. They later became known as the Rosicrucians.

Over many centuries, the alchemists in Europe Have produced many important texts of wisdom. Many of them are decorated with wonderful drawings and diagrams which contain the secrets of Alchemy within a system of symbols that bear interpretation. The wisdom of Caballa has been intermarried into the Hermetic literature, teaching modern magicians the correspondences of planets, numbers, colours and a system of magic based on the belief in angels of the Hebrew religion. Many modern magicians study the art of gematria, which is based in the numerical values attributed to the letters of the Hebrew alphabet. The allegorical art of the Splendor Solis illustrates the stages of the alchemical process, both physical and spiritual. Such magnificent volumes are invaluable reference for today's magicians, and yet can be frustrating to serious students of Alchemy who become locked into a pattern, ever striving for spiritual perfection that they can nearly reach. Yet they cannot help but be aware that if they should take to the lab and attempt the chemical transmutations, there is a piece to the puzzle missing that virtually guarantees failure.

One of the followers of Paracelsus, Gerard Dorn, made a major contribution to the European tradition of spiritual alchemy with his assertion that the first condition of the Work is the integration of the self. He stated that the alchemist should 'Never look outside for what you need, until you have made use of the whole of yourself.' It would appear that he was very close to realisation of the nature of the prima materia, the philosophical mercury for which the modern alchemists continue to strive, that which the Egyptians simply call, *heka*, which is in its receptive attitude in the nature of woman.

In the end, enchantment is merely ritualized Mesmerism.
- Jules Bois

I was under the distinct impression that humans were just animals no different from any other animal except that our society and language are more complex. What useful stuff did we leave behind? Excessive body hair? Obvious mating signals?
- Diablo Verde

Chapter Three

Enchantress

There is no way around the fact that, no matter how liberated the society, daughters are usually far more protected than sons. This can be very frustrating to young girls who are just beginning to discover their natural ability to charm adults, quite often to the extent of usually getting their way on everything except the realm of personal freedom. They are told by their parents that they will understand someday when they have children of their own, and this is true, but this concept is meaningless to a thirteen year old girl who wants to go out with the older teenagers or to go on other adventures which she will likely be prevented from enjoying due to parental control.

Many young girls with a predilection for some form of magical ability will find this particularly baffling when they try their best to get round the restrictive parent to no avail. The art of enchantment comes naturally even to most very little girls, and those with the good sense to keep their tempers in check will charm the adults from an early age with a spell that is peculiar to girls and very magical in nature, although many people do not recognise the magic at work.

Enchantment is effectively the imposition of one consciousness on another. One would not suspect a young child of consciously practising such arts, and indeed they are usually not conscious of it at all. Yet they do it by nature, because it is in the nature of the female to beguile. Many feminists deny this aspect of the female nature and will consciously avoid the tactic, seeing it as somehow unethical. In this they deny an important aspect of femininity which, in a less developed society, would be considered a simple survival technique. Independent women of today may argue that the survival aspect is no longer required and that they prefer to maintain their independence rather than relying on the male of the species, and this is a valid point. However, it does not change the fact that the art of enchantment is inherent, or that it is useful in many other circumstances than gaining a life mate to depend on. It also doesn't change the fact that the underage female is in a situation of dependency on parents or carers whether she likes it or not (and she usually doesn't) and the skill is a necessary technique for getting round the restrictions which are put on her for her own protection, so that she may practise some of the independent adventuring which is also inherent in her nature.

Anyone who has cared for both genders of teenagers can tell you that girls are far more trouble than boys as a general rule. A few hundred years ago, a girl who had reached the age of sixteen would have been expected to be married and producing children as well as managing a household. She may have been legally dependent on a husband, but in actual practice she had her own sphere of influence and the husband would either have been away at war, or influenced by his

wife's opinions in more domestic matters including government if he was active in that sphere. The independent nature of a girl at this age is no different now than it was then, yet parents find it difficult to imagine their teenage daughter managing her own small flat when she can't even manage to clean her room.

However, those girls who find themselves without carers at this age through various circumstances, more often than not will adjust quickly to the need to take responsibility for themselves. They will seem to 'grow up' suddenly, sometimes to the surprise of those who knew them in more sheltered circumstances. There are exceptions of course. In these days of drug filled streets and teenage prostitution there are many holes in society to fall through. Yet these holes are created by the society itself when it fails to train young women for self-sufficiency, preferring to regard them as children to be protected until they are older. When the protection is suddenly removed, the young girl is unprepared for the steep learning curve to sudden adulthood and must sink or swim according to her own inner resources.

Society changes, and with it the ways in which any human skill can be utilised will change. However people don't really change that much. Ask any modern tarot reader what questions their clients ask and they will concern much the same subjects as were asked of the fortune tellers hundreds of years ago; money and fame, revenge, and especially romance. It is romance that will most often concern the young female one way or another. Even before puberty, girls generally become fascinated with attraction. The first stirrings of this interest are not actually sexual in nature, but a fascination with the art of attraction itself. The girl who has a predisposition to magic will naturally experiment with this art in various ways. Often she looks for techniques to attract the attention of boys who are too young to take much notice. This may end up in platonic friendships, the girl satisfied of her success as it was only attention she sought anyway. Friendship is one form of attention.

Later, as she reaches puberty, the same internal methods she discovers in childhood will be employed to attract the attention of boys who are also getting older. However, through some cruel twist of planning or accident the biology of humans is such that girls mature at an earlier age than boys, and all too often the boys of her own age are not ready to become 'boyfriends' yet. This can be frustrating to the young girl who is knocking herself out to attract a specific boy's attention, only to find that he becomes confused and distances himself from a girl whom he may have otherwise liked. She may have been a childhood friend, then she suddenly seems somehow 'dangerous'. His instinct may well be to retreat into his immaturity and claim that he 'doesn't like girls'. He will change his mind in a couple of years of course, but a couple of years seems a long time at this age and the young girl craves attention now.

Several things may possibly happen at this point. The girl may be lucky enough to have an older brother who will bring home friends, and she can turn her attention to an older boy. This can bring its own frustration as boys of 14 –15 may well be interested in girls, but usually the 12 – 13 year old sister of their friend isn't what they had in mind. Exceptions occur when the girl appears to be older than her years, but this can lead to a different sort of trouble as the teenage boy is becoming very aware of his sexuality at 15 while the younger girl is not yet ready to develop her own. Her ability to beguile may seem very sexual in nature to the observer at this stage, yet it is not. I've seen a 10 year old girl beguile an audience full of adults with what appeared to be a very sexual approach while playing the part of Tallulah in a primary school version of the play *Bugsy Mallone*. In real life, the girl was completely innocent and although she found it amusing that her performance got quite a reaction from the adults, she only partially understood why. Her blossoming acting ability had mixed with her inherent talent to beguile, and this created an illusion that the drama teacher encouraged for the sake of its unique effect on her performance. The reaction of parents ranged from amused interest to trepidation. Many found it rather disturbing, as their recognition of the potential in the performance to attract an element of paedophilia conflicted with their appreciation of the acting talent required to pull off such an illusion.

Girls who experiment with magic will usually try some form of love spell at some point. I have only tried anything of the sort once in my life and lived to regret it, but for the average adolescent, this may well be one of her first semi-serious magical experiments. It is at this point that many girls are drawn to the path of witchcraft rather than ceremonial magic, as most love spells come from basic folklore and are associated with the craft of the witch.

Love spells were also popular among women in Ancient Egypt. Egyptian magic contains love spells for bringing a lover into one's bed in dreams. Papyrus 3329 in the Louvre identifies the sorcerer with the god Horus who evokes in turn the divinities of Heaven, Earth, the Waters of the Underworld and the four points of the compass. The invokation runs as follows: "Come to my house this night and open my eyes to (name of desired lover) because of the words with which I invoke you. Quickly, quickly!" Egyptian women from all social classes expected to marry young and to bear children as early as possible. Those who were above the poorest classes had some leisure to concern themselves with romance, and many Egyptian documents indicate that Ancient Egyptian men were often concerned about their wives' ability to stay faithful to them. In fact, property in Egypt was inherited through the female line, as that was the only way to ensure a direct blood relationship between parent and child.

Egyptian love spells consisted mostly of potions, which of course must be drunk by the subject. This is not always an easy trick to pull off. Similar spells have filtered through the ages and have ranged from pleasant concoctions to the most vile brews, but not much evidence determines whether such potions were ever very effective. More effective are the basic sympathetic magic spells which are performed through an object which has some connection to the subject, and this applies equally to revenge or telepathy spells as to love spells. Of course, performing magic through such an object opens channels both ways, so the magic user is left open to backlash through these methods.

My own early experiments with magic leant more to asserting influence over events which were happening in my life. This may be because I've had a very eventful life, and although I was as prone to becoming besotted with one lad or another on a regular basis throughout my adolescence as any other young woman, I found the art of enchantment quite useful enough without resorting to formal rituals, which I was more inclined to do either for more difficult purposes, or for their own sake to discover the extent of what I could actually accomplish with them.

Enchantment is the art of the maiden, yet it is not lost to women as they grow older. Those who master its essence in youth will retain the ability to employ it as need arises. So how is this enchantment accomplished? It lies in an ability to project and to alter the aetheric force, what the new agers would call the aura. Science has never managed to bottle this particular substance. The ability is inherent in the female and it is in her nature to use it, even subconsciously. To deny this is to deny much of what makes us women. I can hear two arguments against this theory immediately. One from the many men who are able to project their will in a similar manner, and the other from women who find themselves unable to master this art easily. The difference between the male and the female application is that it is in the nature of the female to master the art of fine tuning their own aetheric force to become compatible with that of the subject. It is a subtle difference, but an essential one. The father who finds himself wrapped around his little daughter's finger believes himself to be responding to big innocent eyes and his own natural love for the child, yet he is as dizzy and helpless as the lover who looks into the sexually mature woman's eyes and similarly finds himself willing to do nearly anything to please her. The art is almost vampiric, yet unintentionally so.

A trained male magician may learn to impose his will on another, but to draw the subject in so that they want to do your bidding is the art of the female. It is a wordless art, passed from mother to daughter without conscious teaching. Those women who feel themselves bereft of the ability are very likely the product of a maternal line which has lost the skill through cultural conditioning. Women who become victims of extreme cases of patriarchy can have the skill beat out of them, sometimes literally. In the classic story *The Hunchback of Notre Dame*, it is the priest's fear of his own attraction to the gypsy Esmerelda which drives him to persecute her for being a witch. This aspect of this story is a reflection of a situation which has occurred far too many times throughout history. Those women who have missed the unconscious teaching from their mothers still have the inherent ability, and some will discover it of their own accord, but others may need to revive this facet of their nature deliberately.

Learning how to use it consciously is a matter of trial and error more than anything else. It can best be tapped through empathy, not only with people close to a woman but through pets or any creature that she encounters. Those who find it difficult to become close to people at all may well get better short term results in practice with animals, providing that they have a liking for them. A close pet is best, but the gentle creatures in a children's petting zoo or passing friendly cats around the neighbourhood would do. As she strokes the creature, or if she is relating to a person, during any form of close interaction, she projects affection not so much at the subject as into them. Then she immediate relaxes into becoming one with the subject, sharing her essence and emotions freely rather that forcibly. Women who are emotionally inhibited may find this difficult at first, but it becomes easier with practice.

Emotion can make some people feel vulnerable, and that is why the practice subject should be someone or something that the woman feels free to love without restriction. Then, as the woman learns to relax into giving freely of herself, she attempts to see the world through her subject's eyes, to become aware of their point of view and how they may see the woman who interacts with them. There are some women who have had emotionally crippling experiences of life who will find this far more difficult than the woman who simply didn't get the example from her mother, who may have had her own experiences which prevent her from exposing herself to the vulnerability of freely given emotion. These women may find at first that they retreat into defensive strategies, especially if dealing with a human subject.

The biggest error that women make in this regard is in attempting to evoke the ability through false personality adjustment. Attempting to 'turn on the charm' in an insincere fashion is more likely to inhibit the natural channels, although I do always recommend to those who are born with a volatile temper that learning patience and self-control will get better results in most situations. There are few things less charming that a defensive female in a rage.

The other common mistake is to equate enchantment with sexual allurement. Although there would seem to be a connection, especially when a sexually mature female is in the act of enchanting, the abilities are actually quite different. Egyptian Temple Priestesses were known to sometimes bestow sex as a spiritual gift, and we all know that sexuality has a strong effect on the male. But remember that enchantment itself is not based on sexuality. The two may well be employed simultaneously, but the charm of a girl child is not sexually based. It will even be interpreted that it is in her innocence, but little boys are just as innocent yet lack this elusive quality of the female child.

One important fact I must point out is that the fledgling female magician is not limited to the art of enchantment by any means, there are many arts of magic that the more enthusiastic student of magic can discover for her experi-ments. I have brought up the art of natural enchant-ment in this chapter because this is a natural magical ability that is more likely than not to be a starting off point for many a female magician. These days, the role of the maiden may well reach far into adulthood in that a woman is not required by western society to marry and raise a family by a specific age. She may well choose to enjoy her youth and freedom to choose her own lifestyle, even choosing to support herself and maintain her single status throughout her adult life. The other phases of womanhood may intermix with her maidenly status, which is not determined by the presence or lack of virginity. Originally, the term virgin which is often equated with maiden meant an unmarried woman, one who belonged to no man. A free woman, independent in her own right, still fits this description. She may even choose to live with a partner and still maintain this status, while another woman may fall into the maternal, nurturing role in a similar relationship. The difference is one of attitude, rather than one of 'official status' as determined by the records office.

Enchantment can, however, become a factor in other areas of magic and that is where the female magician differs from the male the most. People and animals are not unique in being subject to spells of enchantment, they are only the most mutable subjects and therefore good for practice. The same ability to cast a part of her essence forth and tune into a living being can also be used by the magician to attune herself to a series of events or a seemingly inanimate object or structure. In other words, the female magician can effectively use her talent to beguile toward anything which she might want to affect with magic.

Many are not aware of their ability and so make no attempt to use it, while some perfectly mundane women will 'baby along' the malfunctioning printer at the office, always managing to get it to perform one more time when no one else can get any joy from it. They may joke about her magic or the special relationship she has with the machine, but few mundane people will recognise the very real magic which is being employed. Women who perform spontaneous magic in this way tend to also be well liked in their sphere, whether or not there is any obvious reason why.

The female magician who is very much consciously aware of this ability can apply it to her magical practice in infinite ways. While her male counterpart struggles along to force the changes to happen through arcane formulae and appeals to forces from Spirit, she may effortlessly cast her will forth in her own right, effecting the change with all the elegant and graceful power that a mother wields to 'make everything better' for a child, or a female alchemist employs to effect subtle changes in the alchemical process of transmutation. Perhaps this will give us a hint of the even greater power that a mature woman may access when she commands the power of nurturing magic.

It's out of fear that we respect him. If we didn't he'd ruin our crops or make our prize cow fall ill and die. So I've heard...
- Diablo Verde

Our work is the conversion and change of one being into another being, as from one thing into another thing, from debility to strength...from corporeality to spirituality.
- Nicholas Flamel

Chapter Four

Nurturing Magic

The first thing people often think of when one mentions nurturing magic is the Mother. This is not restricted to those who follow a triple goddess path. It is a common imagery to most people who have known the love and protection of parental devotion, as well as to some who, for one reason or another, were deprived of maternal caring and may have longed for it.

The maternal role has traditionally been associated with this mother imagery, and brings to mind thoughts of comfort and kissed bruises. Naturally, nurturing magic goes comfortably hand in hand with healing magic. However, the nurturing role that women instinctively fall into has potential beyond the self-sacrificing icon of virtue that we think of as 'Mother'. And some of us may have learned when we grew up that mothers have their own needs as well, and may not always act as unselfishly as we once imagined.

In *The Good, the Bad, the Funny* (*The Mouse That Spins*, London: 2002) Ramsay Dukes gives an example of the mother type, describing her as one who will be supportive and helpful in order to encourage dependence of others toward herself. While this example is not very complimentary on the surface, I have come across an alarming number of women who fit the description. They will be the ones who cook the banquets and organise the details of events in a way that puts them in control so that everything is done exactly how they want it, and anyone who offers to help had best be prepared to do her bidding rather than offering alternative suggestions to any of her plans. She will be ever so helpful and will listen to all of your problems, then tell you exactly what you should do to solve a situation. She may get very offended if you decide to think for yourself and maybe make a different decision than the one she has laid out for you.

Obviously not all mother types fit this profile, I certainly would not want to demonise nurturing. I have come across an equal number of women who are true nurturers, who give of themselves freely without any visible expectation of a return. They will organise the same events as the nurturer in the above example, yet will manage to do so without grasping control in the same all-consuming manner. She organises efficiently and brings out the best of anyone involved so that everything falls into place, and the most talented of them can even make it all happen so artfully that she may seem to do it with a fraction of the effort which is actually required.

Surprisingly, I have caught myself in the nurturing role too many times. I've asked myself how this could come about. I started out well, as a typical lazy, useless teenager who left my mother to do the housework and to fulfil my needs while I was blissfully unaware of hers. Many years later, I find myself taking the responsible roles; keeping supplies in the house, making sure we have clean dishes and that the rest of the house is just about clean enough to keep the health department from breaking down the door, and following up on things that are supposed to happen like getting everyone in the family to dentist appointments and seeing that the cat doesn't starve or get locked in a room somewhere. When I try to work out exactly when this transition occurred, I am at a complete loss. One might speculate that we learn by example from our own mothers, which would mean that there is hope yet for my own teenage daughter to grow into a self-responsible adult, yet it is in her that I've seen the inherent nurturing qualities that start so early in a girl child's growing nature. Her natural inclination to look after the smaller children even when she first started school didn't come just from my example. I never had her generosity.

Women who follow a magical path of any kind will find many opportunities to express her maternal side, and this is perhaps one of the reasons that many women choose Wiccan paths which honour the role of High Priestess and Earth Mother. Women who choose the path of Magician instead may not recognise their nurturing instincts as easily, as this is essentially a solitary path. Yet it is in her nurturing instincts that a woman will often find a particular connection to magic that has been lost to many. Those women in chapter two who have practised alchemy devoted something uniquely female in nature to their experiments. Perhaps the same caring attention to the Art that one might devote to a child, or a kitten. When a woman takes on a nurturing role, the object of her interest benefits from a magical touch, similar to that which a mother gives her child when she takes away the hurt of a small injury. There is something all encompassing about this form of magic, to an extent that would seem vampiric if it weren't for the generous, giving nature of it.

Some women who are not consciously inclined toward motherhood will express their maternal role with friends, or a pet. I once knew a happily childless woman who referred to her cat as her 'baby substitute'. While it is true that not all women desire children, the nurturing role is inherent in the female and the astute magician can look for the benefits of this attribute without sinking into a self-sacrificing mentality which may indeed not be a part of her nature.

One of the things I must credit to the feminists of the 1970's is that they helped women in general to have choices. Assessing the need for a family has become an option for modern women, rather than the requirement that it once was. Not all of us are suited to it, or have a desire for it. Yet we need not fear that having a partner or even children will cast us irrevocably into a role we may find limiting. We have the freedom to define home, partner, children, job, etc. in whatever ways do suit us, and in ways that will harmonise with our own self-interest.

Despite this freedom, many of us find it all too fulfilling to be helpful to others simply because we can do them some good, although there is no return in it for us. An example immediately comes to mind. I once knew a mentally ill lad whom I helped with some editing and shared a friendship, knowing there would be no return and that he would eventually turn on me as he did his best friend in school. In a situation where I had some extra stress in my own life, it was actually therapeutic for me to give of my time and experience to him, although I knew he was bi-polar and in the end, as I predicted, he rejected the friendship over an imagined slight. This process was helped along by a jealous mother-type like the sort described above by Ramsey Dukes. She was a mentor to the lad who felt competitive with any other female who came into his sphere of influence, and toward me in particular because of an unwarranted fear that I would usurp her role in his life. There was no danger of this in actuality, not only did I have no desire for the position but his loyalty and love for her were absolute. But jealousy knows no logic and it was further exacerbated by my success in writing which was one of her unrealised ambitions.

The experience of helping him served a purpose for me. The temporary nature of the association didn't matter, the inherent desire to nurture found an expression and distracted me from the source of the stress in my own life. Within this statement is a warning to women, and an explanation of why so many who are not magicians fall into the self-sacrificing role of the mother to the exclusion of all else. A woman who does not have her own interests and who devotes her entire life to the care of family can become immersed in the caring role so much that she virtually has no existence of her own. It becomes like an addiction, and it is these women who suffer from 'empty nest syndrome' when the children are grown and who become almost desperate to find someone to care for in order to define themselves as a person.

There is a danger for women who find themselves in relationships with very controlling men. Some insecure men can prey on her nurturing instincts and use them to take away her independence, insisting that she give up any lines to independence that he feels threatens his absolute control of her. Women have been duped into selling their houses, turning over their bank accounts, losing contact with close friends and family or other lifelines that allow any source of freedom from his absolute domination. Such men display irrational jealously of anyone, especially male friends, that the woman may talk to outside of his own close circle. One of my ex's even tried to prevent me from buying postage stamps because he wanted to know everyone I wrote to and when I was doing it.

Such relationships are unhealthy and are based solely on his insecurity. They generally don't last, and the most astute woman will recognise the symptoms early and strengthen her ties to independence rather than giving in to his demands. This will topple the relationship sooner, but it is well worth missing out on whatever she sees in such a partner as the relationship is doomed anyway. Too often a woman who seeks to heal whatever has caused the insecurity in him will be drawn in by her own nurturing instincts and a little at a time, she becomes enslaved by her own compassion. She cannot leave him as it would surely destroy him. Such a destructive cycle can be difficult to break.

Nurturing does not have to be a weakness. It doesn't even have to be self-sacrificing. It can in fact, be one of a woman's greatest strengths.

The female magician can use the power of ultimate control over her surroundings as an obvious benefit to her magic. The same capability that makes it possible for her to multi-task and maintain the wider awareness of all that is happening around her in mundane life can be of real benefit in her approach to magic. Again, there will be women who read this and immediately dismiss any possibility that they should be so talented. There will be some who look around at their cluttered or complicated life and think that they have no control over their life at all. There will even be some who have lost home, children and self-respect to the degree that they do not feel power in their life as a woman at all.

Yet these same women, if they look around objectively at their life, will find that in fact they do have a great deal of influence over their immediate surroundings. Some of them are using it to self-destruct all too efficiently, but the power is in their own hands. All they have to do is to make a solid decision to change the direction of their life and plot a course to follow, and nothing can stop her from succeeding. This is why four times as many men commit suicide than women. A woman who tries to accomplish a goal and meets obstacles is more likely to find the will to conquer them, or a way around them. The despair of powerlessness comes more to those who subvert their life to the man in their life than to those who struggle to survive on their own. Women are resilient, and very capable of finding inner strength when it is most needed.

This is an inherent trait of the mother. Nature created resilient mothers because caring for a child requires such inner strength and reserve. Look at the animals in nature and how the mothers nurture and protect their young. Which would you rather stumble across in the woods, a bear feeding or a mountain lion protecting a den of kittens? At least with the bear you have a 50% chance that he can't be bothered.

Perhaps the strongest magic that a woman does wield happens when she becomes a mother. The same ability she has as enchantress to attune her life force to beguile a father or a lover is then turned to caring for her young, and the kissed bruise really does stop hurting because of her magic. It isn't only her outward care of the child that creates the special bond between mother and baby or even the fact that the infant grew inside her body. A mother casts a protective shield around her young child on a magical level which creates a bond between them. It does not require a conscious effort, but is instinctive.

This can be inhibited by the mother herself and result in a colicky baby, but in ordinary circumstances it is a natural instinct of which she may be totally unaware. As a magician myself, I was able to recognise and be fascinated by the subtle energies at work when I had my first child. I was later able to sense similar aura manipulation in other mothers, so that it became a bit of a study. Even listening to mothers with grown children as they talked about episodes of their offspring's past stirs up tendrils in their own aura, ready to reach out and connect with the errant progeny, and if necessary protect them from dangers they have long since traversed.

In our most recent generations, we have a situation where women magicians as well as witches are raising children with a conscious intent to teach them about magic. This too is an aspect of nurturing, to teach our children all of the survival skills that we know. Magic, like cooking for oneself, is a life skill to be included. However, as it is a fairly recent phenomenon in our culture except among the hereditary families, we are having to learn by trial how to go about teaching this skill. It can be a real challenge to find the right balance between allowing the child to come to magic through their own volition and teaching them those things which we believe or practice like any other parents.

Sadly, I know many parents, especially among Wiccans, who keep the magical aspects of their lives away from their children when they are very young, so that they will not repeat things in school that will culturally separate them from the other children. There is a certain practicality to this, yet there comes a time when a child is ready to learn some level of magical philosophy.

Raising the magical child is perhaps best done by example. I have known new parents who plan out how they will teach magic to their growing offspring, only to learn from the child themselves that children learn when they are ready. Living in a magical household where conversation is not severely limited will naturally lead to questions as they reach the growing stages where they are ready to absorb the information.

For example, when my own daughter was five, she initiated a game wherein she would choose a colour as she was about to go to sleep at night and I would tell her of the correspondences that would be associated with that colour. This was something that she found interesting, and which I was not concerned about having repeated. Other children would no doubt find the game interesting from a child's point of view. There was no element of religious fanaticism in the village where we lived, which made life easier.

Nurturing magic can be as destructive as it can be productive, just as the same can be said about nurturing itself. One of the more difficult lessons I learned in my young days was to never, never invoke a fertility goddess against a mother, even with good reason. There is always another approach if there is need to use magic against another person. Even in this case, which I mentioned briefly in Spirits of the Fire, it was an act of nurturing, of protecting a friend against an ex who was trying to use their shared child as a weapon against him, that led to a magical error of judgement which resulted in my house exploding into flames during my first experience of a progression spell. The build up of energy was enormous, but the mistake was in my choice of deity. I took the lesson in good humour, but I will never forget it.

Years later, I was able to put this destructive side of nurturing magic to good use for the benefit of my own child. When your child is threatened, most mothers will do whatever it takes to protect them. On this occasion it was a matter of the child's biological father using a legal system that he had financial access to when I did not, to psychologically abuse the child. This is not an exaggeration, he was threatening her on the telephone to take custody and cut her off from access to her mother if she did not say to him that she loved him. It's amazing that he never worked out why she did not. His track record of similar abuses was already well established, including having kidnapped her the first time when she was seven.

The entire story is a bit long for this chapter, but suffice it to say that it was at this point that I had had more than enough and pulled out the progression spell formula that had ended in such disaster so many years before, but with the benefit of many more years of magical experience to refine the approach. The spell itself reversed and changed polarities of traditional correspondences in order to disrupt the natural order of things, such as that the lawyer always wins, and invoked the dual aspects of Hathor and Sekhmet. This time, my choice of deity was very appropriate to the purpose.

The end result was that I could do no wrong in handling my own legal proceedings. Every underhanded trick the lawyer tried to pull was thwarted, and even getting all of my evidence thrown out on a technicality did him no good. Instead, it demonstrated to the judge exactly what had been going on. The judgement was like something out of a film, I was not only given sole custody but there were extra concessions, like backdated child maintenance, that I had not asked for.

It would never be collected of course. Almost immediately afterwards the battle would start all over again when another ex-partner conspired with my daughter's biological father to accomplish a second kidnapping. It was an act of revenge because I didn't fight to keep him when he had an affair with a disreputable woman and asked for a divorce during the run up to the court proceedings, yet he has the audacity to wonder why I was happy to be rid of him. But the victory of the moment gave me the confidence to take it yet a step further when my daughter was kidnapped the second time, and to put a stop to her father's ability to hurt her ever again.

I actually felt a bit of pity for the next man who threatened me with legal action. He had no idea of my previous court-room experience, and despite having known magicians, was not one himself and could not have understood the residual forces that would be up against him even if he had known the story. In an attempt to effectively extort money from me over a very minor difference in opinion over something I had written in an article, he threatened the delicate financial balance that I had established in order to properly care for my daughter while still recognising time as an equal resource to money. I was earning just enough to maintain that balance while giving myself time to write, with a view toward later financial rewards for that effort.

I never quite got to the point of deliberately using magic in the situation as the hunter almost immediately became the hunted and a situation was established where I could not possibly lose anything regardless of what happened in court, and he would have lost more by winning the case than by losing and possibly paying off my debts for me. I felt the magic hanging in the air though, revived and waiting. I've wondered if it may have been that which pushed him to give me so much material for a counter-suit, although it may have only been his own uncontrolled temperament. I will never know for sure, and in the end I let him back out and even agreed to a minor concession to allow him to 'save face'. I have never understood the male tendency to equate money with ego, but the importance put on it and the fragility that was made all too obvious told me of reasons behind it that happened among strangers before I was born, and with visions of Sekhmet's paw holding a mouse by the tail, I decided that I had no need to do him further harm despite his deliberate nastiness to me.

And that is where the real power of nurturing magic finds its strength. One who is really in control of a situation does not need to prove it by completely destroying the opponent. The children are told to "say sorry" and play nice from now on, and the world is right again. I advise anyone who uses the progression spell method to keep this in mind when applying it, regardless of the nature of the situation. Progression spells were explained in *Chaos Monkey*, as well as in a two part article in *Chaos International* issues 24 & 25, but I will include the method in an appendix for this book as well for those who haven't seen the previous publications.

In this and the previous chapters, I have broken out of the PC mould and emphasised that there are forms of magic which come naturally to women by virtue of our gender. While this is certain to ruffle a few feathers, it is also a recognition of the simple fact that men and women are indeed different, and gloriously so. These differences extend far beyond the obviously physical and into attitudes and approaches that may be cultural influences to an extent, but some of which are inherent. This will continue in more chapters as we look into the nature of women, especially women of magic, we creatures who for many centuries have been depicted as mysterious and unfathomable by male writers. Sometimes, these depictions even paint us as creatures of the dark.

To Know,
To Will,
To Dare,
and to Keep Silent

!!! How dare you be repentant! How dare you!
What little pitiful little respect I had for you has now been
washed away by
Your unashamed apologies!
For shame...

- Diablo Verde

Chapter Five

The Mysterious Dark Feminine

Women are often attracted to that which is mysterious and forbidden. There is something about those things which are considered 'dark' which is uniquely feminine in nature. I am aware that there are many 'white witches' who will disagree with this assertion, but the magicians I write the book for will immediately recognise the truth of it. The young woman who is attracted to 'a bit of rough' in her early relationships, or who is attracted to the occult despite a likely objection from family, demonstrates this aspect of femininity. In patriarchal societies, it is this that many fathers and husbands see as some sort of weakness in the female, who is naturally attracted to that which they see as forbidden. In extreme

cases of some religious societies, women are even considered naturally drawn to evil.

Most men will admit that they do not understand the workings of a woman's mind. In very authoritarian societies, men will actually fear women because they do not understand us and feel they have no control, even in their child daughters. Many books on the tarot say that the card of the High Priestess in the Final Outcome position indicates that the future is not to be revealed, but less often do they explain that this is because it may well change because the situation has a delicate balance in operation that may go one of many possible ways depending on subtle changes from various causes. The woman who understands this card completely will know that she has the power to grasp control of the situation, and to tip the scales in whatever direction she chooses. The woman magician may also realise that to do so is a risk, and only in trusting completely to her deepest intuitions, rather than what appearances tell her, can she hope to tip them into her best interests.

The old saying, "A woman has the prerogative to change her mind", is a recognition of the flexible and naturally chaotic nature of her thinking processes. The same adaptability which allows her to multitask also gives her the ability to change direction in response to changing circumstances. It is part of her resilience and an important survival skill in an environment where she is considered to be the weaker sex and therefore a potential victim. Another saying is "The female of the species is more deadly than the male." It is the feminine, the yin in forms of martial arts that recognise the balance of male and female energies, that allows the flexibility required to respond quickly and to think on one's feet. Watch untrained brawlers and you see that the men fight in a very linear and clumsy fashion by nature, while the women assess the opponent for weaknesses to exploit.
This same survival technique is applied to other situations

such as business or even daily life. Men will often lament that they never know what a woman is thinking, or that she changes her mind easily. We become the mysterious, the unknown, the unfathomable...when actually we had just moved on to the next thing we need to do.

The realm of the feminine is traditionally that which is dark or hidden. Naturally, the occult (the word actually means hidden or unknown) is a realm where a woman's nature thrives. Even in the fluffiest of Wiccan circles, the High Priestess with any modicum of magical awareness will instinctively gather up the combined forces of all the participants to direct the magic they raise. It is in her nature, and it is the reason that it is the Priestess even in a balanced group that has both priest and priestess who will perform this task.

In magic(k), this power of women can be well employed or it can be exploited. Too often the potential of her abilities is missed in groups where either sexual awareness of her becomes a distraction, or the good intentions of political correctness try to deny her unique femininity. As a result, many woman magicians choose to work solo or are less effective in the group than they might be.

It is not unusual for woman magicians to look into the darker mysteries of magic. Study of any kind within the occult is likely to be of interest and of potential use, and those who are not severely conditioned by past religious taboos will find an easy understanding of the mechanisms behind forms of magic that even within the occult community, are often deemed as dangerous or forbidden.

The reasoning is that flirting with the dark side doesn't make you evil. It just makes you informed. The balance of nature holds both dark and light in an interacting whole, and a woman's attunement with this rhythm and balance is constantly invoked through her fertility cycles. Despite the modern day perfume and make-up culture which masks her more primal nature, there is a part of every woman that is wild and untameable and which is naturally drawn to secrets and hidden information, often for their own sake. It is this which brings her an attraction to darker magic, and to the understanding required to master it effectively.

Women have a reputation for being emotional creatures. This is well deserved, yet it is within this emotional nature that women can find their unique affinity to magic. In modern chaos magic, a fair amount of emphasis is being put on the use of invoking emotional states which can be employed in ritual. It is a method which delves into the deeper human psyche, our most primal inheritance from ancestors who practised magic in shamanic trance states through which transition could occur on a spiritual level, which necessitated manifestation on the physical level. It is basic in structure, yet ultimately effective.

The Dawning Of Chaos

In studying the various magical paths, we come across references to dark goddesses from many mythologies. Some of the names will be familiar to anyone who has any experience of paganism of any kind; Hecaté, the Morrighan, Sekhmet, Lillith, Kali, etc. There is a certain fascination with these goddesses that leads some Wiccans to admonish their group members to avoid them as they are considered dangerous. For the same reasons, many others within the magical communities form an affinity with them. There is seductive-ness, and sometimes an attraction once again to that which is dark, secretive, and therefore powerful in a particular way. If one looks into their actual mythologies, what will often be found is that these goddesses are often associated with the secrets of fertility, with protection of children, and sometimes even with creation of all life as is the case with Tiamat.

Tiamat is a chaos creation goddess who gave birth to many entities, now recorded as demons, and was eventually conquered by a male god of order, Marduk. Her mythology follows a common theme, and exists in various versions from the countries where we get another variation on this theme which has grown into modern Christianity. One of the common threads in this theme is that all begins in unformed chaos, and when life takes form, there is a woman to give birth to it. Often to the gods themselves. But then she is pushed aside or conquered by a young male, shining in the Sun, who takes credit for her efforts and becomes the saviour god. There is plenty of material for both goddess religions and feminists to work with in these mythologies.

Working With Dark Energies

The mythologies associated with magical paths are of importance to the more religious paths like Wicca, but the solitary magician more often looks at them from an anthropological point of view. There are some who align with a specific goddess in their practice of magic, and any of us may invoke one that suits a situation as I invoked Sekhmet and Hathor for my custody battle. But the real purpose behind such an alliance is to tap into the emotional states within that are associated with the chosen deity figure. It also provides an external catharsis point into which to find the right balance of emotion and self-control.

There is a knack to invoking an emotional state, and yet maintaining a cold detachment to the ritual itself, especially if it is intended to affect a situation of great personal import-ance to the magician. This was one of the more important aspects of the most intense magic I ever did, which was in relation to the child custody situation to which I've just referred. The legal battle which was to be the subject of the spell gave rise to some of the most disruptive emotions that a mother can experience, yet the spell itself, like the courtroom, had to be addressed dispassionately in order to be effective.

Quite often it is when a woman is pushed too far so that her emotions have reached a point where she no longer cares about consequences that she is able to reach such a state. I had the advantage of my calm, Scorpio nature and many years of magical practise to help impose the required self-discipline before reaching that extreme. It didn't help that the partner I had at the time chose the run-up to the court battle as a good time to ask for a divorce. He later admitted that it was a selfish bid for my attention, which was focused very much on rescuing my child from her abusive biological father. But that selfishness made it easy for me to effectively brush his intended interference aside and tell him we could sort out the legalities when I returned from the all-important battle. The detachment needed for the ritual allowed me to feel absolutely nothing about the broken relationship. All of the history behind it, all of the emotions that had been involved in the various stages of its history at that moment became as dust, swept away and forgotten.

That level of detachment can be reached more easily than many women may realise. What is required is a situation of greater importance, when the thinking facility is of paramount importance to survival and the emotions. While never actually either mastered or transcended, the volatile emotions are actually pushed aside like conscious thought in a yoga meditation. They are not suppressed, but are temporarily ignored in favour of the necessary action to do something constructive about the situation; mundane, magical or both in concert. This is magical discipline.

Nature gives us the facilities for dealing with stressful situations. Just as hunger raises energy and intuition in preparation for the hunt, danger or crisis evokes hormones and brain enzymes that can be constructively put to use for survival or quick thinking to deal with any situation. The mental states that we reach as a result of these natural chemical reactions from our bodies have been used in shamanic magic for most of human history, and can be refined in the magician who is consciously aware of what is involved in the process. Even fear itself can be utilised in magic, and this is where some of the methods like sacrifice of life have their power.

I am not suggesting that animal or human sacrifice is necessary to magic, there are plenty of ways to invoke fear in our modern world. But this is a historical aspect of darker magic that should never be forgotten. Some dark goddesses, Kali for example, are well known for demanding human sacrifices. Yet she has never suffered for lack of worshippers. Even today, when this form of worship would be unthinkable in modern Western society, there are many drawn by fascination to her and who seek other methods of placating her in their modern form of worship. Sometimes, just the fears evoked from her bloodthirsty history are sufficient to evoke the required reverence in her modern followers.

But blood and sensationalist tactics are not inherent in what is considered to be 'dark' magic. Much of what is considered to fall into this area of magic is a matter of breaking taboos, delving into the deeper realms of the mind, and questioning, perhaps overturning, the conditioning that has been instilled in us from society. Sex magic is often included in the definition of 'dark' magic for precisely this reason. These are qualities often seen in Trickster mythologies. They are also commonly practised in various forms in modern chaos magic, which is known for deconditioning and using the subconscious mind in particular for effective magic. Sometimes to get a result in magic, you have to upturn the status quo a bit, as I did when I refused the consensus reality that 'the lawyer always wins' and won as a result. The look of surprise on his face alone was worth the effort.

I've met quite a lot of female chaos magicians. Chaos magic makes use of the subconscious mind, and as a result attracts the internal nature of a woman. While chaos magic is not inherently a 'dark' magic, it often gets painted as such because it utilises any form of magic that will get results, and often this breaks free of the generally accepted 'white' magics that the public face of paganism have on their 'approved' list. This is just as well, as chaos magic can be more than a little disruptive to the life of the magician, and adaptability is a basic survival tool for those of us who choose this path. Riding a wave of chaos is no picnic, and yet it is uniquely suited to the female temperament which is inherently emotional and adaptable to internal changes at every change of the Moon cycle. Yet part of the deconditioning process for the female chaos magician is to develop the knack for taking control of the chaos rather than riding with the roller coaster of constant change. This is no easy task to master, and the lessons can be unmerciful.

Dark magic is not limited to cursing or negative intents as its reputation would sometimes portray. These can certainly play a part, but any intent in magic may be approached through the realms of the hidden or the deeper psyche. Sometimes a ritual method may be painted as dark because it reverses the ritual methods of an established religion, thereby breaking taboos like the Trickster and deconditioning the mind of a magician who may have been trained in childhood to adhere to the particular religion.

Some solemn ceremonies in major world religions hold an element of power of which most of the church going participants are largely unaware. For example, in some parts of France it is believed that if three Catholic masses are performed simultaneously on the same day, that a magician who positions herself at the exact centre of the triangle formed by the three locations and working in synchronisation with the ceremonies can cast a very powerful, perhaps even fatal spell. This is an obvious holdover from Christian superstition, yet the concepts of timing and location are valid in that the power matrix thus formed would create serious magical possibilities. Arranging such a situation could be complicated, particularly because a priest would be unlikely to knowingly co-operate with such an operation and co-ordinating three such priests would be nearly impossible except by timing the ritual to a common time on a Sunday morning when these ceremonies generally take place anyway. The ritual would be just as effective if the magician were central to the locations of any other established religious rituals which were being performed simultaneously.

Sinister associations have been made to magics that use effigies, figure made of wax, wood, clay or even metal impregnated with something taken from the subject's own body, such as hair or fingernail parings. Yet these basic practices go back even to ancient Egypt under the Pharaoh Ramses III. In Egypt, they were most often used for love spells, yet are just as effective for revenge or healing magic. It was the women who most often used these spells in Egypt, although there is more of a mix of male and female use in later religions like voodoo and the use of poppets in British witchcraft. The magic is considered 'dark' because of its very power to have an effect on someone from a distance, and especially through their own bodily substances which may have been collected without the subject's knowledge. In many societies, distant magic has been associated with women as they have had to rely on it when it was the men who wielded swords or other weapons for protection.

Yet it is a similar form of magic that is used in a protection amulet, perhaps placed on a child. Amulets can be charged with a number of intents and given as gifts, but protection and healing are the most common uses for this type of magic, using an object to transfer the magic created in a charging spell to another person through a material medium. This begins to look less dark to the observer, despite the similar nature of these forms of magic. Magic itself is an unquantifiable force, and therefore of the hidden realms. Often referred to as the 'dark arts', magic is only measurable by observed results which are unlikely to be repeatable under scientific conditions, and therefore will remain mysterious and dubious to mainstream society.

This, in itself helps give magic its power, just as there is power in secrets. A secret is something that becomes suppressed, and as a result begins to affect the subconscious mind, and this is why many old spells admonish the magician to remain silent as many old folk spells require that the magic user must not speak to anyone after the spell until a final act, sometimes as simple as walking a number of paces, is performed. It is basic sublimation at work, the same method that is employed in modern sigil magic wherein an intent is symbolised with a sigil which is destroyed and effectively forgotten after the charging spell.

Some mystery is retained in the old formulae whereby a magician worked in a protective circle. This is continued in modern practice more out of habit than anything, although some recognition is given to the value of creating a magical space for ritual. It was considered important in days when the invoking of spirits was steeped in religious superstition and a separate space, traditionally a triangle, was put outside the circle for calling up nefarious spirits to force to one's will. This practice has been effectively discarded in modern magic and replaced with the familiar pagan circle of protection. Fear gnosis invoked in the act of raising an unruly 'demonic' spirit might be approached with a more educated attitude now with a recognition of the mechanism in play, or the practices may be occasionally revived by people new to magic who find the old formulae in books, but working with spirits is more often likely to consist of calling them up as the protectors of a circle in modern magic than as something to fear. A magic circle cannot protect you from something you evoke into it.

The woman magician, working alone, may or may not bother with such a circle at all depending on her background and personal practices. A magical space is likely to be established in some way for ritual, but the circle itself has largely become either a pagan practice or a social demarcation in group magic. Any large group of people who want to openly interrelate naturally form into a circle. It is used in story telling, in support groups, and around campfires among other things. Its use in magic no doubt evolved from such social gatherings.

Information about various magical practices has become widely available in our age. A woman can join an established magical group, start her own, or study alone and experiment with her own methods. It is not necessary to choose and follow a single 'path' in magic, although membership in a group or Order may influence the direction of any individual's practice during their association with that group. Women still fill a minority among most magical groups, and as a result are often coveted as members. They are also more likely to quit a group long before they are able to advance in the ranks, but we will discuss groups in a separate chapter.

The availability of magical information as well as the changes in society brought about by the 1960's sexual revolution has created a climate where women are able to define their own personal and magical ethics. Despite the greater understanding of psychology and human nature that has developed over the years, this social freedom for women has actually served to increase her mystique among her fellow magicians.

There is more to this than a reaction to her sexuality. Like the little girl mentioned in chapter three, the woman magician has a beguiling effect on all she meets, which is actually enhanced by the renegade association which is made to her independent status if she works solo. She stands apart, like the High Priestess card in the Tarot, and this quality will remain with her in her relationships, even when she works with a magical partner.

One touch, and I was lost in you
Sinking into the dark pools of your eyes
Falling forever into an oblivion
Of that which transcends passion
Knowing you as I have known no one before

- anon

Nice people always have something they want, and it's usually
unpleasant...

- Diablo Verde

Chapter Six

Magical Partners

Ideally, a magical partner is most often also one's sexual partner, although this is not always the case and not always possible. The two main reasons for this are that the close relationship on both levels intensifies the magical potential, and it avoids complications with separate sexual partners who all too often experience jealousy to some degree or other of the close magical relationship.

Many people will intentionally combine their relationship with a sexual partner with their magical life for these reasons. Whether this is actually good practice or not is for the individuals to decide. I went through most of my life without having had a magical partner, despite having had relationships with men who practised magic in some form. The reason for this is that I need something more than a

70

sexual relationship to work magically with someone. Only twice in my life have I experienced that 'something more' from another person. It is a natural connection that could never be forced, something which feels as if the other person is vibrating on the same frequency as oneself.

This first happened to me with a close friend (who could never have been a sexual partner) on our first meeting, at the touch of fingertips as I handed him something. It was an intense and powerful experience, and I had to intentionally break a contact which I really didn't want to relinquish because I felt myself sinking into him, losing my sense of individuality and becoming as one magical force. This all occurred within a few seconds, unnoticed by others around us. Eventually, the magical intensity between us made even the friendship impossible to sustain, party due to outside circumstances.

A magical partnership with someone with whom you also share a sexual relationship has its challenges, as relation-ships have their own patterns and most people can never entirely separate their personal life from their ability to respond to their magical partner in ritual if they are still dealing with the same person. As a solo magician, I have very little personal experience of the difficulties that occur when a couple is experiencing stress in the relationship and trying to ignore it for the ritual, but I have seen it happening among people I know. It is a distraction for everyone involved in the ritual.

I have had the experience of attempting to work with a partner from a very different path. Whether this could work for someone else may be possible, as some paths are more compatible than others. In my experience the attitude of the partner was that I should forget everything I had learned about magic over more than thirty years and blindly follow his lead, never asking questions. Of course as a chaos magician one of the inherent aspects of my own path is to question everything, and most of all what mechanism is behind any act of magic that makes it work. The end result was that we couldn't work together at all, and eventually the rest of the relationship followed a similar pattern and came to an end. Lesson learned.

Couples are not always able to work together magically, especially if they follow different magical paths. However, I do know one couple who work perfectly happily in their separate groups, and are very blissful together. I think that to a large extent it is the personalities of the individuals that make the difference. A sexual partner who is not a magical partner must be able to maintain respect for that which is a part of the magician and to give her space to practice her magic, or a conflict will surely arise. Living with someone who constantly tries to subvert your practice and convert you to following their own ways is much like an occultist living with a religious fanatic.

The key word there is 'follow'. Women who become magicians are not generally followers, although there are some exceptions who will inevitably look to a group to give them a lead and become devout followers of that group's practices. I once actually accused a woman of waving her pom-poms for a particular Order that had allowed her to join, as her enthusiasm for that group as the only right group was much like the sycophant. This is not to say that all women in groups are followers, far from it, but some women magicians will inevitably look to a group to support her efforts, particularly when she is new to magic and needs a starting point. In the case of the pom-pom woman, her approach was so much like a religious convert that I couldn't take her seriously as a magician. In general though, women who choose the magical path have an independent nature and this is going to have an effect on their relationships, both personal and magical.

Different Planets

It is worth taking a look at how men and women relate to each other as partners before relating that to the effects it has on their magical partnership. It is not considered 'politically correct' these days to acknowledge that there are inherent differences between men and women, yet the best selling hardcover book in the 1990's with the sole exception of the Bible was *Men Are From Mars, Women Are From Venus* by John Gray. It was actually on the Best Seller list for four years. Both men and women can recognise that they are indeed different, especially in the ways they communicate with each other, yet most don't understand in exactly what ways.

I did not read the book, but I did see a television documentary based on it which demonstrated through several volunteer couples where these patterns of different communication emerge. One of the first things I noticed about the programme was that all of the chosen couples were typical suburban family examples. Some of the wives worked outside the home, others were full time homemakers. There were situations which universally applied to these couples which do not necessarily always apply to 'alternative' or magical couples, who often live outside of the 'typical' mould. However, some worthwhile insights were demonstrated on the programme.

Having experienced both the roles of the stay-at-home housewife and mother as well as the working wife, I could see the common elements that affect both of these roles and which also carry into alternative relationships. Many of the stresses caused by the suburban roles are avoided in less traditional family structures, yet the basic differences in communication and understanding of the other gender often still apply.

One of these differences is the perception of affection and romance. One of the biggest mistakes made by the husbands on the programme was to buy large and expensive gifts for their wives and to expect that to make up for little things, like an affectionate touch or a spontaneous gift of a wildflower. John Gray suggested to the men that a woman should be touched non-sexually at least ten times a day, just an affectionate stroke or caress, to remind her that he loves her. Small spontaneous (and often inexpensive) gifts had more impact than buying the woman a car or a holiday in the long term. The men could not understand this, and so Gray put it in terms of different perceptions from species from different planets. The men became Martians, the women Venusians.

I actually found myself sympathising with the men in many parts of this programme, as the stay-at-home wives had largely become tyrants in the home and acted far too much like mothers toward their husbands. Her perception was that he worked for only a few hours outside the home while her role was 24 hours, and he could help her with the children or other household tasks when he walked in the door. His perception was that he had done his day's work and could come home and reap his reward of relaxation. Most of the husbands went straight for the television when they came home. This is part of a 'Martian' pattern where he withdraws under stress into a private space (sometimes only a mental one, where the clutter he steps over doesn't exist), but would get lonely eventually and come out for company, looking to his wife to be glad to see him.

This pattern didn't sit well with the working wives for a different reason. She came home from work, also wishing she could relax, but would need to start cooking or taking care of other household tasks and would resent having to do it all herself. Some would terrorise their husbands into helping with housework, expending twice as much effort to solicit his help than it would take to do the job herself. Of course if he actually did something to help, instead of appreciation he would most often get criticism for not doing it properly.

It is not to take the man's side in this resentment cycle that I report his side of it, but to point out the differences in perception that were uncovered. One of the problems that men had was equating affection directly with sex, and then becoming confused when the woman asked for more affection, yet would only have sex with him infrequently. In the follow-up to the seminar it was found that those who made a point of touching and cuddling their wives non-sexually on a frequent basis as a result of what they had learned found that their sex lives became much more frequent and improved. By giving the Venusian what she wanted, he received what he was after in the first place. There had to be a lot of give and take. Much of it came down to giving her more apparent attention in small ways. Showing her that he thought about her when they were apart during the day made a big difference. Bringing her flowers for example was not a material need, but one that showed that he thought to do it. Having to ask him to do it negated the entire effect.

The women were taught to ignore the Martian cycle and leave him alone when he withdraws, confident that he would come out again when he was ready. They also learned that a simple thank you for things that the husband did would guarantee more assistance in future. Simple appreciation for any little task done had too often been withheld, yet made a real impact when she made this small effort.

Another important point of different perspectives was a woman's need to rant about her stresses, whether they were work related or over spending a day at the mercy of demanding children, or even over something unusual that had happened during the day. The woman's need was to rant, the man looked for why he had to listen to it and wanted the bare bones information about the situation so that he could see what he could do to help her. In most cases there was nothing he could do to actually help and she wasn't looking for that. Establishing that fact validated her feelings and acknowledged that it was indeed an unsolveable problem, and therefore she was satisfied. The man is still confused as to why she needed to tell him when he can't actually do anything. The Martians are geared toward taking action, while the Venusians just need a sounding board.

Many men find it difficult to simply listen to a woman, and will shut down. If she realises that he isn't listening, she gets upset about that on top of whatever it was that she was ranting about.

The only cure I've found for this discrepancy is to recognise that sometimes we don't listen either. As a writer, I wander easily inside of my own head and can all too often shut out things that people are saying to me that don't interest me (which is why I hate taking minutes at a meeting). Once when I was talking to a partner he was caught out not listening, but had the courage to admit it and even said that he was sorry that he hadn't been listening. The defensive body language told me that he was expecting a bad reaction, probably based on what would have been forthcoming from his previous partners (I've met two of them and can imagine).

However, I calmly said to him that it was probably good that he did that, because I sometimes do it too and if we understand that quality about each other, we needn't get upset about it. It became a bit of a joke after that. One of us would catch the other not listening and simply confess, "Sorry I wasn't listening again". That "again" has to be in there, to remind us that it's something we acknowledge as a natural trait of creative people, which is easier to accept than a gender divide. It worked, just as acknowledging that we were both very solitary people who needed a certain amount of time on our own works. Having that time allowed us to fully enjoy the time we spent together and each other's company, because we had already satisfied our individual needs for solitude.

Taking it to Magic

Similarly, magicians who work with other magicians in partnership, regardless of the nature of their relationship, can benefit greatly by recognising patterns of communications and individual needs. If they are male and female, there is a high probability that some of the insights discovered by John Gray will be demonstrated between them. Whether or not they share a sexual relationship, the actual communication patterns are likely to be shaped to an extent by their gender, especially if they spend much time together. A platonic magical partnership can slip into the behaviour patterns of a married couple all too easily, which is something I've also noticed among role players when they are coupled in their roles.

In the magical relationship, her affection needs would seem to only be relevant if they are also in a sexual relationship. Yet she does need to have frequent appreciation for her role as magician and what she can bring to that, just as he still needs to receive recognition for any good contributions he makes. In these days of open goddess worship religions, the crossover with magic(k) can build an association as can the association of traditional male and female roles, which can lead to one partner or the other taking the lead in ritual. Magicians work best as equals. One or another might take the lead in a specific ritual which they have written, but this needs to balance if the working relationship is going to remain in balance itself.

Magical partnerships work best in an atmosphere of mutual respect.

Abusive Relationships

There is no room in magic for abusive relationships. They do happen, and on some level a certain amount of magic is possible through them, but it is not sufficient to justify the abuse.

Women have a history of subjecting themselves to far too much indignity in relationships, some more than others. The worst case to come to mind in my own experience was a woman I met once among hippies in San Francisco. She was a pathetic spectacle of a woman, who completely lacked self-respect. She talked of how unattractive she was and how she knew she wasn't worth anything because she was fat (she had a bit of a tummy, nothing extreme), and of how desperate she was to keep her relationship with one of the men in the group who was rather nice looking. Within a week of my only meeting with her, he left her. I never saw her reaction.

Many women reading this will immediately say 'It couldn't happen to me', but who among us hasn't felt foolhardy love for an unworthy man sometime in our life? Is there any woman who hasn't in some way, at some time, behaved completely stupidly as a result of this? Perhaps someone very young. Such devotion has driven many a woman to everything from humiliation to acts of crime and even suicide. While I am a strong person by nature and have not reached that extreme, I have had one mentally abusive ex who gave me a lot of insight into how this works over time.

I've had a few short-lived relationships that might have gone in such a direction if I had allowed it, but by nature I resist any attempt to subvert my free will and easily walk away from these attempts. This one was an exception for a few reasons that with hindsight I can see how it happened. First of all, there were qualities about the man that strongly attracted me in the way that one can get enthusiastic in a new relationship. Secondly, he had been badly hurt by his first wife which caused me to put up with things that I would not ordinarily endure because I didn't want to exacerbate the damage. This, I decided afterwards, was not my responsibility. We learn from our mistakes.

Physical abuse is easy to identify. A woman can say that if her partner ever raises a hand to her, she will leave him, and stick to it. Mental abuse is more subtle. It often isn't apparent in the beginning of a relationship. Worse, the memory of the time when he behaved better will often keep a woman in a relationship in hopes that he will revert to his previous apparent personality. But slowly, a little at a time, he seems to change. The subtle difference between being knowledgeable about a situation and taking over when you have ideas of your own, can escalate until you reach a point where even expressing your opinion about what you would like to watch on television becomes a major offence and any independent thought about magic certainly meets with criticism.

Obviously this is not workable in a magical partnership. It isn't workable as a relationship in any aspect, but it is particularly unworkable in a magical setting. A woman can be completely subservient if her only goal is to serve a male magician as an Altar or assistant of some sort, but to be a magician of any description requires a degree of strength and individuality, not to mention the freedom to express one's own imagination and magical ideas.

This also works the same the other way round. A woman who finds a man who will defer to her in all things is in a position as High Priestess, which is appropriate to some forms of witchcraft and Wicca. The path of the magician may take many forms and there is certainly room for partners to agree roles on a temporary or permanent basis that may not be completely equal, particularly in forms of sex magic that may involve S&M, but completely subsuming the personality of another person is not working in partnership. Even the High Priestess is in a leadership role rather than one of partnership unless the coven works with Priest and Priestess together as the older forms of witchcraft do.

Platonic Partners

Although it is less common, magical partnerships may be formed with other people that are definitely not romantic partnerships as well. In this situation, the gender or sexual orientation of the partner is mostly irrelevant to the actual magic. Any potential for raising jealousies or complications with the romantic relationships that the individuals have outside of the magical partnership must be considered and dealt with to avoid distractions, but within the magical partnership itself the disassociation from tumultuous emotions is actually an advantage. I would even go so far as to say that the balance of closeness and detachment that a platonic pair of magicians can reach during the magical state itself is something for romantically involved couples to strive for while working their Art.

As I explained before, it is possible to meet someone whom you immediately feel yourself attuned to closely on a magical level. If an association will not cause disruptions in your other relationships, what begins as a friendship may easily become a magical working partnership. Some may say that the magic is sufficiently important to override any other relationship complications, but it would be a mistake to underestimate the effects that emotional entanglements can have on the magic in progress.

Another consideration is whether the magical relationship and the closeness it engenders might possibly give rise to a sexual attraction which otherwise might not have occurred, at least with any strength, and whether that would create problems at any level. Closely related to this is the factor of possible sexual magic practise. While not everyone works with this, those who do must consider whether the magical relationship can remain platonic if the participants practise together, or whether in this partnership a limitation must be drawn to avoid either internal or external difficulties, if not both.

There are no precedents for formalising a magical partnership regardless of the relationship between the participants. In the case of a High Priest and High Priestess working together in witchcraft or Wicca, some traditions may have been established in specific paths, but the path of the magician is individualistic by nature. Even the established Orders are more likely to bestow advancement on working partners separately according to their own attainment within the group hierarchy. Two individuals (or more, as we will see in the next chapter) who choose to work together magically outside of these formalised structures can benefit from consciously deciding what parameters or conditions they wish to work within together. This would include the nature of the relationship between them and what form they both wish for it to take. If they wish, it would not go amiss to perform a formalising ritual together to dedicate their work or speak phrases and even vows as to their intent in the partnership. As I said, there is no precedent for this, but there is a beneficial psychological effect to such a ritual as a rite of passage which might be equally compared to a wedding or an initiation. It marks a transition in the lives of the individuals to a new phase of working collectively.

The important thing is that any two people who make the decision to work as magical partners communicate effectively from the start so that they have the same expectations and understanding of the partnership between them. This is especially important for a female magician, and even more so if the partner is a man, regardless of the sexual orientation of either of them. Misunderstandings and hurt feelings can be avoided through mutual clarity of purpose.

Two or even three people can have a very close and intense magical relationship which is very different from larger group work. This might be said of a small group of people who work together, but the dynamics are different than in a direct magical partnership. Such close relationships will have an effect on how the partners relate to other magicians both as individuals and in groups where one or both partners may be a member.

In these days of easy communications, it is very likely that a woman magician in particular will come across other magicians. As a member of a minority group, most women will find themselves quickly invited to magical events once their existence becomes known. For the woman, there are quite a few rocks in the ocean of the magical community that she will be faced with negotiating her way around. Whether it is right or fair that it should be different for her than for a male magician is beside the point, the simple fact is that she will be regarded differently when dealing with other magicians.

Life's a game;
There are the players,
and there are the played.

- anon

That's dumbing down though... removing the hard parts. They
did that with my GCSE's, we had to learn matrices, then in
the year I do my GCSE's they drop matrices from the syllabus.
Gits...

- Diablo Verde

Chapter Seven

Women and Other Magicians

Magicians come in a diversity of paths and beliefs. Most in the modern climate have learned from various paths of magic(k) and eventually settle into a direction that suits their own personality. Occasionally you may still meet someone who claims that a specific path is the 'only real and true' path to magic. I encountered a statement of this sort in a book written by a known author on magic who claimed that the angel magic popularised by Dr. John Dee was the only real magic. My opinion of the author as a magician immediately plummeted. While this area of magic is well worth study, and I do have some rare texts concerning Dr. Dee on my shelf, there is a broad diversity of magical paths to be discovered beyond any one historic magician's teachings or discoveries.

Personality cults abound in the magical community, some of them are quite widely spread. It is up to each magician to choose whether to become involved in one of them, but she should be aware that others exist and that the lessons of history and of magicians of the past are only part of the discovery of magic. Quoting a favoured magician verbatim does not confer divinity on the followers. Learning the key phrases, however, may prove valuable as a learning exercise.

Encounters with other magicians who have strong opinions about their own path of magic is to be expected. Ideally, the magical community strives to rise above differences and to respect the opinions of others. Discovering what path you are best suited for can take some experimentation, and this may include participating in groups and associations that will ultimately be not right for you. It is all part of the learning process, and should not be considered a failure if a parting of the ways eventually results.

The woman magician should not be discouraged if she encounters sexual dynamics, group politics and outright 'bitchcraft' and ego from others as she finds her way through the labyrinths of the magical life. While these things are not inevitable, they are common enough that being prepared for the possibility can help to avert disillusion. People are people, and they have human frailties. Magicians are not above their own humanity.

The flip side of this is that magical groups and associates can be incredibly supportive. Having many friends in a diversity of paths myself, I find that even just socialising with others who have an interest in some form of magic fills a social need to be able to discuss matters pertaining to magic with people who at least know what you are talking about. I am very open about magic at my 'day job' and in all aspects of my life, yet there is a definite difference in being able to attend my local moot and to discuss magical ideas with other people, even those who follow a very different path than my own.

I have worked with a variety of small groups and individuals, which span Wicca-based groups to Chaos Magic groups, and have found some value in all of them. The majority of my friends are either witches or magicians of various persuasions. This can be a bit limiting to other aspects of my life, yet it is the result of a natural progression over time, that I would become most social with people who share this interest in some way.

Relating to other magicians as an individual with my own thoughts, beliefs and ideas might easily be compared to a social group of artists who relate to each other. They each have their own speciality and talents. Their work is often very different. But they share the same core interest and some aspects of the art will be common territory for them, at least in the basic mechanics of how things work. How they perceive the way it all relates to them personally is an individual experience, yet it results in a unique experience that each can appreciate in the other.

The subject of women esoteric artists recently arose on an e-list in which I participate. The list is primarily focused on the art and magic of Austin Osman Spare, but as on all such lists, the conversation deviates regularly. One person asked why there were not more women artists like Rosaleen Norton whose art has been compared to Spare's on many occasions. Immediately several people offered website URL's for women they knew who created esoteric art in various forms. They have been among us all along, quietly getting on with it as women magicians tend to do.

One of the major differences I've noticed between encountering other women magicians and encountering other women in the wider pagan scene is that there seems to be no need for competition between women magicians, while at least half the women I've encountered in Wicca groups tend to immediately try to place any new women into the pecking order. I say half because it is not universal, and hopefully my friends within this community will recognise the sort of individuals I refer to and know that it doesn't apply to them personally.

Often, if a woman feels the need to be in charge of a group for any reason, it will lead her towards goddess worship religions where the woman plays an important leading role. The woman magician is likely to be more solitary in her magical practice, even if she chooses to join a group at some time. When I've encountered other women magicians, both solitary and in chaos groups, the dynamics have been completely non-competitive. There was more of a mutual curiosity and interest, and a sharing that reflected the ideal of sisterly affection. It was a recognition of someone else that was more 'like us' than most other people we've met with an interest in magic of any kind. The last time I started practising with such a group the first comment I heard from one of the women was "Oh good, more girls!"

Another woman in the group lent me a robe, and so it went. Quite different from the last time I was introduced to a woman leading a Wicca group who immediately assumed that I would want to join it because I had two friends who were members. She behaved as if she were worried that I might usurp her position as leader, when in fact I had no interest in the group at all. I find that women magicians tend to be self-assured as individuals in general, which can be intimidating to less secure individuals. There may be exceptions, I have known a couple of women magicians, by e-mail only, who seemed otherwise and put a lot of importance on the groups they joined as if they looked for their self-identity within the approval of other magicians. Those I have met in person through other friends or at events that tend to draw 'our kind' exude a quiet confidence that I find unique in character. While I know male magicians who certainly have a similar confidence, the subtle nature of the woman magician is recognisably different, probably at least partly because her experience of life will be from a woman's perspective. They also exude the allure that I explained in chapter three, which does have an effect on women as well as men.

Male magicians that we meet react in a variety of ways to a woman with confidence. Some find it fascinating, while others may find it intimidating. My last ex, who was a Wiccan rather than a magician, admitted more than once that he was frightened of me and the effect I had on him when we first met. I have also met male magicians who react with respect, regarding the woman magician as an equal without having to work at being 'politically correct'. This is particularly prevalent among my gay magician friends, who often tend to be chaos magicians (although certainly not always).

Sexual dynamics can be very distracting when mixed with magical dynamics. Even gay magicians have a habit of reacting socially different to a woman than to a man, but for the male magician whose natural instincts when meeting a woman is to at least subconsciously assess her sexual attractiveness, reacting to her as magician rather than as woman can require a little extra self-discipline.

One of the things I find as a woman magician is that I am frequently asked to join groups. Although there are many more women magicians around than many people realise, groups tend to draw a majority of men and so they will often seek to recruit more women to their ranks. This can be a problem when the invitations come from friends, especially if their path is not entirely compatible with your own. More than once I have had to turn down a close friend, with whom I was more than happy to share ritual, when asked to take an oath that I felt was not suitable for me personally. In one case I refused a very old and traditional oath, because the wording included dedications that I was not prepared to adhere to. It caused some temporary strain in a close friendship, but in the end my friend respected my position and the love and friendship continues still. I respect him highly as a magician, we just follow different paths.

As in any magical path, close relationships can overlap with magical associations and sometimes they will be compatible, other times they will not. I mentioned in the previous chapter that I know one couple who are wise enough to recognise the magical differences between them and practise in separate groups. I know many more who try to compromise, but the compromise is to their relationship as well as to their magical lives. This often happens because a romantic attraction to someone can lead us to try out their chosen path. It can work similarly in a new friendship. You meet someone whom you like and they are practising with a group and invite you along.

This could potentially be a good situation, perhaps an opportunity to learn a new area of magic or discover a group that will suit you. But difficulties can arise when you decide that the group is not for you and you seem to suddenly lose interest. This can create a complication in the friendship with the other group member if they feel slighted by your withdrawal from the group. This kind of awkward situation is becoming less of a problem as time goes on and magicians learn to respect each other's differences more, but it does still happen.

We, as women, will always draw the responses that people have to women. This varies a great deal depending on whom we are dealing with, but it is human nature to respond differently to the different genders and no amount of feminism will ever change the reality of that, nor should it. The only change that being a magician brings to it, is that they will also respond to us in relation first to their personal response to the realm of magic, and secondly to the apparent deviation from the mainstream that is perceived of a woman who follows the magical path. By and large, I find that the response from other magicians is one of respect. Ironically, the biggest exception to this appears to come from within some of the oldest established magical groups, but we will deal with groups in the next chapter.

A woman who travels the path of magic(k) does not stop being a woman. If she develops working relationships with individuals, they will respond to her differently because she is a woman. It is a fact of life that we must accept. Resentment gets us nowhere. Probably the most important thing a woman magician can learn in relation to her magic is to fully appreciate her qualities as a woman and the unique abilities that she can bring to magic as a result. When she fully embraces her femininity, she is able to access the power that goes with it.

I personally have always seen the advantages of womanhood. There has never been a time in my life that I have seen it as a hindrance or wished to be a man. I have also never considered myself to be a feminist, although my independent nature might lead some to assume otherwise. I have simply refused to take patriarchs seriously, even before the women's movement of the 1970's. From earliest childhood, I've recognised advantages to 'being a girl' as the old song says.

Sometimes it is very much an asset. If she works with a small circle of friends, say three to five people, the nature of a woman is likely to cast her in an influential role. If the close associates are all female, they will either form a natural sisterhood or will fall apart through competition. The natural empathic qualities of the female have the potential to form very close-knit ties with those with whom we feel able to allow to be close to us.

The dynamic, however, changes when we associate ourselves with a larger established group or Order.

That's a tad harsh. The man just wanted to know about authors, and you suggest he douse himself in mace and run screaming into the night stark bollock naked trailing lobsters from his arse! Harsh man...

- Diablo Verde

Chapter Eight

Women and Magical Groups

Historically, magic in the Western world was a man's game and magical Orders were created and dominated by them, yet many of them in the nineteenth century and afterwards had female members. Aleister Crowley's famous quote, "Every man and every woman is a star" reflects the acceptance of women as magicians. The frequency of female authors on the articles in his magazine, *Equinox of the Gods* demonstrates a recognition of their value. The Golden Dawn was known to have had a woman as their first initiate. The OTO and A∴A∴ had several female members. However, the leadership roles in these groups continued to be filled by men. Part of the reason for this was societal norms. Women had been taught to fill a subservient role in all aspects of society, and magic was no different. The changes would come in conjunction with changes in the status of women, most notably during the sexual revolution of the 1960's when Wicca and the 'New Age' began to gain popularity.

The Witchcraft Act in England was repealed in 1954, and this coincided with the formation of what became modern Wicca by Gerald Gardener. Using some historical sources, he created a religion where women played a dominate role, some even as High Priestess. The position of women in ceremonial groups was affected by this change in society as well. By the end of the 60's, Anton LaVey had founded the Church of Satan and women filled yet another new role; that of Altar. While many would say that this put women back into a subservient role, women who have been members of the church generally dispute this and claim to have been treated with respect within the structure of the organisation more so than in most magical groups.

Occultism flourished in many forms thereafter, and women gained power in society through various means, not least of them the feminist movement of the 1970's. Wicca continued to grow and to become the public face of the occult, visibly becoming to some minds a women's religion. Women continued to be members of the magical Orders as well, and in the spirit of being 'politically correct', many members of these Orders have tried to work on the basis of sexual equality and some women have achieved positions of status within the hierarchies of the Orders.

Human nature being what it is, this attempt at societal progression has had limited success due to the complexities of sexual dynamics. Progression for women within magical Orders is still often affected by who is sleeping with whom, but not always in the woman's favour. Quite often it is against a woman's best interest to become involved even in flirtation with a member of a group she wishes to join, as this is easily interpreted as the woman attempting to use her sexuality to gain favour, whether or not there is any truth to the assumption. I have known women who have lost credibility through a simple attraction to a group member in this way.

Interestingly, my own personal experience with nearly joining a group was not affected by this sort of dynamic. Much of this I believe to be because of the fact that a majority of the male members were gay. Also, my partner at the time, although a member, did not hold a high position within the group. Ironically, he was promoted at the same meeting within which I turned down the initiation. This has caused me some amusement since, due to the confusion it created among certain 'ranking' members of the group who would normally denigrate anyone who had the audacity to turn them down, yet were unable to follow this course in the company of one of their respected members, who continued to be my partner as well as a member of their group.

Group dynamics are a funny thing. It is a frequent occurrence for personal relationships to cause complications in magical groups, whether these are friendships or sexual relationships. In Wiccan groups there are likely to be a certain number of couples, and a fairly even balance of male and female coveners (ideally) unless it is specifically a men's or women's group. In Magic(k) groups, it is more common to have a prevalence of men.

This creates a situation where complications can arise. Despite the best intents toward equal treatment of men and women, human nature has a way of creating what may be observed to be tribal behaviour, where the women of the group are treated differently in some way by men who often don't even realise that they are doing it. The other women will often also respond differently to women members than to men, perhaps unconsciously.

Many women I have spoken to have described differences in the way they have been treated in well known magical Orders. Sexual dynamics comes into it, even in groups where most of the men are partnered. Men in the same Orders have expressed the opinion that they treat women members no differently, yet the women still insist that these differences exist.

It can be interesting to observe how women react to each other in non-magical group situations. They can be competitive creatures, or they can be supportive. I have been in societies where being an unattached woman is effectively a sin. The coupled women will perceive a threat from a single woman in some of these cultures, for no other reason than that a new woman in the group does not 'belong to' some man. Cultural expectations can form much of how people perceive each other.

One of the pitfalls of the magical life is that groups will attract a certain number of people who are looking to magic to fulfil personal psychological needs rather than purely spiritual development or the pursuit of magical knowledge and practice. This can result in neurotic behaviour from some members of magical groups of all persuasions. I think that anyone who wants to join a group should ask themselves why, and exactly what need they expect to have fulfilled by doing so. There are perfectly legitimate reasons for wishing to work with others, but self-questioning is very basic to magical development and examining one's motivations is always worthwhile. This is doubly true if your desire is to be the leader of a group.

Humans are social animals, and wishing to work with others with similar ideas to your own is quite natural. Group work can also be fun, and some rituals work best with several participants involved. The trick is to find people with whom you are compatible. Some compromise is always required to form any sort of alliance, and a person who always insists on using their own methods to the exclusion of others is likely to become quickly unpopular to work with.

The woman magician who wants to join a group is advised to learn as much as possible about any group that she considers joining. Not only is the history of any well-known group important, but the reputation of the specific Temple, chapter, or group by any other name which she is considering is worth knowing. If there is no way to learn extensively about the group, following her intuition should take precedence over any desire to become a member. Some groups are reputable. Some are not. Any group, regardless of whether its name is known historically or not, is only made up of the individuals who form its membership. Any group that requires only the women to work skyclad or requires only women members to undergo sexual initiation should be considered dodgy until proven otherwise.

While the details of any form of initiation ritual are most often kept secret for good reason, any legitimate group will give honest answers to questions such as "Is sexual initiation required?" I know of one legitimate Order where the answer to this would be 'yes', but it is required of male members as well. Further questions should be asked, even if the woman magician is unconcerned about this form of initiation. Each woman must make her own choices, but self-respect is essential in the magical life, and compromising it for the sake of group membership is always a mistake.

As I said before, one of the biggest mistakes a woman can make is to start a flirtation with a male group member when she is seeking membership. Despite political correctness and all the platitudes about equality, this is still easily perceived as a woman trying to use sexual favour to get into the group. It may be very far from the truth and the other members may deny any such perception, but time and again the dynamics of the group have been affected by this situation. Difficulty can be avoided by waiting at least a little while to become established before pursuing any liaisons within the group.

I have spoken to women who were current or past members of various groups and have found that a majority of them have encountered the sort of arrogance that is endemic of many magical societies. Some of the male behaviour they have encountered was subtle patronisation, yet some translated as sexual harassment in a few of the more extreme cases. The curious thing is that men I have spoken to from the same groups have usually not interpreted the actions of the males as anything but equal treatment. It would seem that they are completely unaware of their actions, or that the women interpret them other than how they are meant.

There would seem to be no easy answer to these differences in interpretation of human behaviour. A woman who wants to be part of a magical group is faced with making one of several choices regarding how she wants to proceed. She may wish to join a well-known Order and deal with the dynamics within that group. If this is her choice, I can only emphasise that she would be well advised to avoid any flirtations until she is established within the group, if only to avoid misunderstanding of her intent or unkind gossip. True that it is not fair that men are not likely to have to be quite so careful, yet a man who joins a group and immediately is seen to 'come on to' the women in the group can face similar ostracism and be interpreted as someone who is only seeking to join a magical group to find 'sexually loose' women.

Another thing to consider is that women can sometimes be oversensitive about unequal treatment, and may forget that men face difficulties of their own. These difficulties may be different for men than for women, but a woman who perceives herself as always the victim of unfairness can often create her own problems and become boring as a perpetual 'victim mentality'. Much of magic involves creating your own world, and refusing to see sleights as inevitable because one is a woman (or any other specific category of person) is the first step in overcoming the obstacles that may occur.

Another approach that women have been known to try is to join a group and attempt to reform their treatment of women in the group. This is a bit of a fool's game, much like becoming involved with a man and then trying to change him to suit your criteria. However, if there is a large percentage of women in the group, some subtle influence over time may have an effect. If the dynamics of the group is very contrary to what the woman finds acceptable, she is better off giving the group a miss.

Which leads to a third choice, she can start a group of her own. Magical groups do not have to be steeped in history to be valid organisations. Actually, starting one is quite easy. A person who starts a group or Order sets its criteria, and only needs to find others with similar ideas of what a group should be to recruit members.

The main drawback of any group is that if it becomes a large organisation, it begins to form a mob mentality. Members begin to perceive themselves as more important because they are members of the Order. This is not a phenomenon exclusive to men, I have seen women affected by the status of being a member of a known group in ways that clearly display their lack of self-love as individuals. My own criteria for a group I would join would probably be that it would have to consist of members who are individuals who feel no need to be part of a group, but are confident individuals in their own right. This, of course, has kept me from joining groups and Orders in general.

We must remember however that humans are social animals. There is also value in sharing ideas, and some ritual methods are suited to group work. Working with a group of like-minded magicians can be downright fun! So, what is the discerning woman magician to do? Most will try group work in some form at some time. Many of these will seek to join an established Order sooner or later. I see this as a healthy experiment, so long as the woman is aware of the fact that any group, even a local chapter of a historic and worldwide Order, is made up of its individual members. Whether any specific group is right for the individual is something she will have to decide for herself, but she should be aware of the pitfalls that can be encountered and at all times, insist on keeping her self-respect.

Some women have chosen to form woman-only groups in order to avoid sexual dynamics in group work, or because they prefer the company of women. The majority of these are Dianic Wiccan groups, which may not suit a woman whose path is more toward ceremonial or chaos magic. There is no reason why a woman-only group of magicians shouldn't be formed. As more women tend toward Wicca than toward Magic(k), members may be few, but that is more likely to result in a closely-knit group.

All groups are subject to group dynamics, which can take the form of competition for group leadership, disagreements in policy and procedures, or differences in ritual style. However, these problems with group work should not be overly discouraging to those who want to work in groups. Joining or forming compatible groups can be as complicated as finding the right relationship. Trying out a few that don't work out in the end does not preclude eventual success in finding the right compatibilities. The larger the group, the more complex the dynamics among its members and the more compromise that must be shown by all in order to make it work, but the success of the group may be worth these considerations.

Similarly, a woman joining an established group must appreciate that these dynamics among individuals will have been worked out (hopefully) among the existing members, and adding a new member will always require some adjustment for all involved. The most productive approach is to try one's best to assimilate the group spirit before trying very hard to impose one's own personal stamp on it. This will come naturally with continued activity in the group.

Human nature and sexual dynamics are not going to disappear because we have ideas of 'higher purpose' or 'spiritual development'. One might imagine that the first magical Orders to allow female members may have found difficulties abounding within their ranks as they encountered the complications that would have arisen. In the Golden Dawn, the early members strove toward celibacy as a spiritual ideal, even married members. This may have suppressed much of the difficulty of a mixed-gender Order, yet suppression of human nature or desire are not conducive to magical development and much of this long since abandoned attitude was based in the Christian morality which was still prevalent at the time.

Conversely, Crowley's A_A_ was reputed to have celebrated sexual freedom, at a time in history when the women would have been 'marked' by such behaviour. In modern times when women may choose their own sexual behaviour, complications remain despite all attempts at politically correct perceptions and we are all too often still judged by our personal behaviour, whether it leans toward promiscuity or more circumspect sexual choices. Either has its pitfalls. The best decision for any woman is what feels right for her at the time, and to have enough self-confidence that the opinions of others are unimportant. However, this is an ideal that doesn't come easily to all. Dealing with group dynamics requires dealing with the perceptions of the other members of that group. One thing to remember is that if the expectations of the group are other than what feels right to you, it is probably not the right group for you. There are others.

This is not easy advice for those who live in areas where there is little magical activity at all, much less a plethora of magical Orders just waiting to be graced by one's presence. I know one woman who lives in a big enough city that there are chapters of most well-known Orders, yet she has made the same mistake with all of them by getting involved with a man in the group too early. This has resulted in a situation where she no longer feels able to practice with any of the local groups, yet feels the need for contact with other magicians. She has dealt with this by becoming part of an on-line community of magicians for social contact, while practising alone. It is not ideal, as she wishes to participate in group work. Perhaps she will form a group of her own someday, possibly even an all female magical Order.

Despite the complications, women should not be afraid to try group or Order membership. It is not like the sensationalist novels, we do not sign away our life in blood before being allowed to attend a first meeting. The group I nearly joined only required me to sign a statement that I would not reveal members' real names. There is no way to enforce it, I don't believe for a second that slipping up on this would carry dire consequences. However, by my own personal ethics I consider this oath binding for life, and also hold confidential anything which was discussed within the group meetings I was allowed to attend. Not much more than this would have been required if I had taken the next stage of initiation, and yes, I do know far more than I'm supposed to about what occurs at each stage of their initiations. At some point I would have been expected to swear a level of loyalty to the group that I would not have been willing to swear, even though that too is unenforceable. I do not take an oath lightly.

Each must make her own decisions, but it is best to make them from an informed position, and to overcome any fears that would prevent experiencing the different dynamics of group work. I hope the advice given in this chapter will help some women to avoid pitfalls, but also that it will not restrain anyone's path to personal experience.

My experience with the above group was a valuable magical exercise on many levels. It happened at a significant time in my life, when I had just accomplished a major magical victory over a personal situation and was considering various changes in my life. One of them was whether to join a group that had drawn my attention for many years. This particular group had been through many phases of its own over time and I had been repeatedly warned off by disgruntled ex-members, but I've never been one to accept the opinions of others, even friends, without looking into something for myself.

Unlike the ex-members, I have no criticisms of the group although in the end I did refuse the initiation. There were some group dynamics involved in the decision, but on an individual basis I still consider everyone I met within the group to be friends at one level or another. It was what had happened to the group structure itself that resulted in my eventual decision to go my own way. The original ideal of non-hierarchy had been lost, giving way to human nature. Organising a meeting for them gave me a good look at how the organisation worked and pitfalls of growing too large.

The time I actually spent attending group meetings over two years was fun as well as good magical experience. While I have no doubt whatsoever that moving on was the right decision for me, I have fond memories of my time with the group and feel it was an important chapter of my magical life. I still have a lot of respect for the members I worked with. Occasionally I am asked my opinion about this particular group. I don't discourage people from joining to see for themselves whether it is right for them.

Group work is part of a natural process for the student of magic. As I've said, the clever female magician who joins a group is well advised to get to know the group without sending out sexual signals if she can help it in the beginning. Establishing herself as a competent magician first can make all the difference. It shouldn't take long for most women to attune to group dynamics, and to establish her place among them. After all, she has the benefit of a woman's intuition.

I don't want a crowd of acolytes. They make a mess on the carpet and get under the feet.

- Diablo Verde

Chapter Nine

A Woman's Intuition

My mother's generation was more familiar than the current one with the phrase, 'a woman's intuition'. In many of the Western cultures of the last century, the fact that women tended to have such an intuition was accepted as folkloric fact (a deliberate oxymoron) and particularly among those who had mothers who stayed at home to care for the family rather than going out to work, it always seemed as though the woman of the family knew things that she couldn't possibly have learned through ordinary means. Especially about what the children were up to.

Some of the reason for this would undoubtedly be a matter of having the time to pay attention, but not every incident could be explained away so easily. My own mother still knows when something is wrong in my life, even from 6000 miles away. While one could argue that a certain degree of psychic ability is inherent in all people, it is women who have gained a reputation for it.

There are a couple of reasonable explanations for this. For one thing, as was explained in an earlier chapter, women are more often than not naturally empathic. If the slightest thing is altered when someone close to her comes home; the child who has had a bad day at school; the husband who has had an afternoon affair with his secretary; the close friend who has just had a break-up with her boyfriend; the typical woman will immediately sense something out of place. She will observe subtle clues, and before you've even said hello she is asking you what is wrong.

This has become less obvious in modern society as so many women are no longer filling the carer role in the family and are often too busy to notice as much as she once would have, yet despite my own very busy life I seem to know if my teenage daughter is having a crisis the minute she walks through the door before we're even in the same room. The traditional roles have changed, but the instincts that went with them are still there. There is an historic reason why we have this ability.

Whether we like it or not, women have most often filled carer roles in society and the family. If we look all the way back to hunter/gatherer societies, we still find the women at home doing the caring and housework while the men are out hunting. Perhaps if you research far enough an exception can be found, but as a general rule the women have been put in this position where they are responsible for the protection of home and children, and have to wait for their men to return.

Waiting is never easy, and some of these women will have found methods of divination to try to predict when or if their men would return. Many more would develop an instinct to sense this, as they were too busy chopping wood and chasing children to pursue the arts of magic directly. Again we come back to maternal protection, which still requires us to sense danger for our offspring. Like the mother animals in the forest who sniff the air and look for any sense of danger before leaving the den, we seek through an internal instinct for any hint of danger any time someone we care about leaves the house without us. We do it without thinking about it most of the time. It may extend to friends or pets in our modern society where not all women will choose to have children or even a mate, but the inherent need to protect anyone we care for is still very much a part of what we are.

This can have an interesting application in magic. The development of this area of empathic ability opens up a 'touchy-feely' aspect of magical aptitude which is one of the reasons that women are often attracted to witchcraft with its spiritual applications. Ironically, the same approach is particularly well suited to the area of chaos magic where sensing patterns is a useful skill. It is also a useful faculty in the arts of divination.

There are a variety of methods that individuals choose to use for divination. Very popular at present are tarot cards and runes. In the old days of the gypsy fortune teller (who were frequently women), cards were used as well as the scrying crystal, or crystal ball. Direct scrying through a ball or black mirror is most often, although not always, easier for women. Edward Kelley was an exception to this, as he used a crystal ball to scry for John Dee. Admittedly the first black mirror I ever used belonged to a man, but the direct scrying methods make use of the empathic abilities that are commonly inherent in women. The images which are reflected in a surface of glass or water, or even in fog as I learned in my younger days, serve to trigger that sense of pattern that lies within.

Interestingly, a black reflective surface tends to be easier for those who benefit from being drawn into its apparent depths than a surface which reflects the brighter light reflections. Nostradamus was known to use a bowl of black ink for scrying, and I do find the black mirror more prevalent among male occultists in general than the classic crystal ball, although many keep one for decoration. My theory for this is that some men have a capacity to let go of the usual need for control which is inherent in their gender in certain circumstances. In my observations it seems to be these men who are both able to use divination effectively, and to give of themselves fully in relationships.

Again, making generalisations, men are often attracted to divination methods that require some form of analysis, such as astrology or the I-Ching. The exception to this is runes, which is a method that requires as much intuitive interpretation as tarot cards. Runes are generally found in use more often among men than women. I suspect, based on my experience of those I know who use them, that this is because runes are often the method of choice among those who follow the Odinic paths where runes are part of the cultural association. The path does attract a high male ratio.

Now that I've covered all of the sweeping generalisations so that those who are the exceptions are probably thoroughly brassed off with me, let me point out that the purpose of this book is not to say that 'women are good at this and men are bad at that', but to point to ways that are particularly useful for women, while still acknowledging that some men are perfectly capable of benefiting from the same methods. There are some very empathic men in the world of magic, and these may even find understanding of their individual magical nature within these pages as much as any woman, without necessarily having to tap into a feminine side of themselves. What I seek to convey are the paths to magic that are most beneficial to women, regardless of whether they are also useful to men, and to open up a new perspective of the strengths of the feminine abilities which transcends the stereotypes and generalisations that have hindered progress in the past.

Once a woman has accepted the potential of her natural intuition, she will want to learn what methods best suit her for accessing her ability. Many things will be known to her

without resorting to any of the physical divination methods available to modern magicians, yet she must learn to trust her instincts before they will be of much practical use. Most women will respond to 'hunches' and feelings that arise from her inherent psychic abilities, yet all too often logic will interfere with a strong impression that cannot be backed up with evidence and she will talk herself out of doing something about a situation because it seems 'silly'. Later on she will probably feel like kicking herself for not trusting her intuition.

Also, some circumstances involve too much strong emotion to maintain objectivity, and this is where divination methods can be very useful. They bring focus, and tap into the deeper psyche where the confusion of emotion has less influence. Women are often suited to forms of divination that require either direct psychic trance state such as scrying or interpretation of abstract forms, such as in tea leaf reading where symbols are useful for helping the subconscious to communicate with the conscious mind.

Patterns with symbols might be found in many mediums; rust, paint spread across a path, the surface of a stone or a pattern on a ceiling can provide material for the subconscious mind to form into meaningful symbols. Methods of divination can be traditional such as using cards, finding lost objects on a map with a pendulum or dowsing with rods, or you may want to try abstract methods like throwing paint at paper and interpreting the symbols found therein.

The right one will vary with each person. I often use tarot, but rather than depending on word translations I find it useful to learn the pictorial symbols and their deeper meanings. They may say something entirely different than a book translation in context of a reading. There are usually many symbols in the cards to draw from, but this can cause overload to those who haven't learned them over time. Something like Runes, which have a single symbol with a general meaning, may be more appropriate for some. Just learning to quiet the mind and sense patterns is essential for someone who wants to practice any form of divination.

Interpreting imagery in these methods is still more of a conscious act that learning to read what Stephen Mace refers to as 'energy flow' (*Addressing Power*, Self-Published, 1996), which as he points out is a distinguishing characteristic of chaos magic. Mastering this ability relies very much on the intuitive faculty, and this is where the touchy-feely nature of the woman who practises magic is very much at home. The woman who follows the path of magic(k) is likely to learn something of the ways of nature in today's magical climate. The general principles of chaos science have become familiar among other groups of magicians than the chaos magicians.

One of the keys to successful practise of divination is to maintain an openness in one's perceptions of the world at all times, rather than just when actually performing a divination. The 'spirit of childlike wonder' that we hear about so often is something worth cultivating because of the effect that it has on the magician's ability to interpret subtle forces and changes in conditions in the world around them. If you watch a small child, they will often show an appreciation of toys that do nothing, such as a snowglobe, yet the slightest difference in their immediate world, for example an unknown person moving near to them in a shop while their attention is apparently focused on some fascinating distraction, will bring an immediate reaction. It is that awareness of changes in conditions that opens the mind to enable it to access information through divination methods, or to direct impressions.

While we're on the subject of impressions, a simple exercise in perception which I actually learned in a psychology class is worth mentioning here. I have not had the opportunity to compare the degree of impressions received through this exercise between men and women, but it would be an interesting experiment to carry out. It is done with a simple full-face photograph of a person. Cover half of the face, and look for clues about the person in their expression, particularly in the eye. Much can be seen therein. Then cover the other half, and see what you can read about the person.

If you're feeling brave, you can try this on a photograph of yourself. It is probably better to try it the first time on a photo of someone else who is close enough to you that you can determine if your impressions are correct. Be prepared for a surprise. I did this with a photo of someone I was to meet soon when a mutual friend offered to show me a new batch of photographs she had just had developed. With this simple method, I was able to tell her extensive detail about the person's emotional history and the state of his current relationship (his girlfriend was also in the photo) that she mostly knew, but I had not known before analysing the photo. She was amazed, although she had heard of the method before. It was the trick of looking at the hidden sides of his personality in the eyes that made the difference. It was during this analysis that I saw a future business relationship between myself and the man in the photograph, which may well be under way by the time these words are released in print.

A female magician has many tools at her disposal. Some of them are also available to men, but her approach to them may be different. However, there are some tools that can only be available to a woman, or to someone who works closely with one.

Of course it's all part of a process whereby you go completely insane and come out the other side, mostly, so perhaps it's not for everyone.

- Diablo Verde

A magician must be able to go without food, without water, and even without chocolate.

- Jaq D Hawkins from *Chaos Monkey*

Chapter Ten

Blood of the Mother

Bodily fluids have often been used in forms of magic. Old folk spells ask for anything from spittle to urine as part of their 'charging' formulae. Ceremonial magics often use a drop or two of the practitioner's blood or even sexual fluids. The one substance that is available exclusively to women or those who work with them is menstrual blood.

Menstrual blood has some unique qualities as a substance that may be used in magic. Part of this comes from its perception as something that is taboo. Women in some societies have been put aside while menstruating as something 'unclean', to be avoided. This, we can assume, comes from the superstitious reaction to blood loss and it's association with death. Ironically, it was best expressed by the character Mr Garrison in the cartoon series, *South Park*, "I don't trust anything that bleeds for five days and doesn't die!"

Modern magicians know that associations with the cycle of sex and death are common to some of the most powerful magics. This is magic based in the most fundamental cycles of nature itself. Creation and destruction, birth and decay, play a part in all that exists in the universe. Magic based on these principles meets little resistance as it fits in easily with the flow of the natural order of things, and yet it has been avoided by many over the centuries because of their fear of this very process, and of their own mortality.

Using menstrual blood in spell creation has often been looked at with the same revulsion as blood sacrifice, despite the lack of a victim. Yet its purpose as a nutrient for growing life in the womb puts it on the other side of the circle of life, as the life giving principle rather than that of death. As a substance, it is easily used as the equivalent of the semen of the male in the sort of magics practised by Austin Osman Spare, who was known to charge sigils with his own semen. In efforts toward political correctness in the magical community, some have tried to equate vaginal secretions with this to adapt Spare's methods to female use, yet the substance is not actually equivalent in that vaginal fluids are used only for lubrication and do not play a direct role in bringing about the spark of life as does semen. It is the woman's menstrual blood that feeds the growing foetus, and which therefore actually contains the creation principle.

As this blood contains the nutrients for bringing about new life, it takes a step beyond providing the first spark that an enthusiastic sperm cell might supply. As a substance in magical use, it symbolises the nurturing of powerful magic. It is of particular use in progression spells which require some patience to mature, thereby growing in potency.

The analytical mind, which is often evidenced in the woman who chooses the path of magic(k), tells us that bodily substances are only symbolic and have no actual magical qualities of their own. Yet their use in magic has proven many times over that they do make a difference. However much we may rationalise that this is a matter of psychological association, the results speak for themselves. Either we are more susceptible to these psychological processes than we tend to be in any other situation, or the substances do have a quality of their own which science has not managed to bottle or explain as yet. Considering the lack of sustained scientific experimentation on the validity of magical processes, this is not surprising.

The use of blood in ritual in undeniably emotive. When you consider that a woman is hormonally put into an altered state of consciousness by the menstruation process, then the idea that using this altered state in magical practice makes more sense than the unexplained superstitions reveal on their own. This part of a woman's cycle can be either the best time for ritual or the worst time, depending on the ritual method and approach. What I do find particularly useful is to use the changes that occur over this cycle to create what may be termed a complete ritual circuit. We know that a woman's mood changes with the changing levels of hormones. There is a noticeable comparison between these altered moods and the changing psychological states during ritual. To the magician, this presents an obvious magical opportunity.

Probably the most intensive sigil charging method I have ever used is very much aligned with this cycle, using a progression spell method. A small circle of parchment paper is cut for the purpose and consecrated with menstrual blood. This sits on the Altar overnight. Often a ritual Altar is set up specifically for the purpose, and kept in place for the duration of the working. The following day, the sigil is drawn on the parchment and a preliminary ritual is performed. The details of this may take many forms, using methods collected over many years of study in magic. The important element is that the intent of the ritual is stated, thereby causing the connect-ion with the sigil.

A simplified form of the same ritual is performed daily over the Altar, working up to the ovulation part of the cycle when a more ecstatic method (dance perhaps) works its way into the daily performance. This settles down into a more repetitive and even perfunctory form as the days move on, until the cycle returns to its beginning. The ritual is formally closed, and if an Altar was set up specifically for the ritual, it is dismantled. The sigil is usually burned in the process of the closing ritual.

Making use of the female's susceptibility to mood changes can be enacted in a variety of other methods as well. Odd as it may seem, using chocolate in ritual as a sacrament is effective because of its chemical properties. These have a stronger effect on the woman magician than on the male, because of the way in which our own body chemistry reacts with the substance. Chocolate contains polythenol which is an anti-oxidant and is good for the heart.

This chemical is also found in green tea, which is good news for those of us who want to avoid the sugar that is added to most chocolate. When preparing green tea, you should not steep in boiling water, but rather in hot water (approximately 160-200 degrees). It is not as effective if you add milk. The Chinese and Japanese believe that green tea is beneficial to health, but only in moderation. It is calming, cools the body rather than warming it like black tea does, and protects against some forms of cancer.

Polythenol is found again in olive oil. The female magician can benefit greatly from learning the connection between her eating habits and her body chemistry. Including foods in the diet that contain anti-oxidants can result in slower aging, easier menstruation, and an overall more resilient internal strength that is a goal of any magician. Apart from chocolate, green tea and olive oil, these anti-oxidants are found in high quantities in red or yellow onions, tomatoes (especially cherry

tomatoes), and red wine. Nutritional alchemy is a worthwhile study for the woman magician, as her body will react strongly to any changes in the diet. One does not have to give up favourite foods to effect changes as can be necessary specifically for weight loss. Adding a few key sources of the right elements like anti-oxidants will bring significant results without any need for a change of body shape.

Anything you put into your body will have an effect on your mood in accordance to how it affects your physical constitution and chemical balance. This is particularly important for women magicians to remember if they want to have control over the body, the mind and especially over the delicate hormonal balance that comes with our gender. This does not mean that a woman has to be a health nut to be an effective magician, only that she will benefit greatly from being attuned to the effects of various nutrients and substances. Magic is a path of personal discipline, but this does not have to translate to austerity. Those who practice methods such as chemognosis might be surprised to learn just how quickly a vitamin C deprived person can reach trance after eating an orange. The key to any form of externally contrived gnosis is awareness, especially of the dangers of delusion in experimentation with any form of intoxicants.

The aware female magician can make use of the chemical changes in her own body in ways that would be very difficult for a male magician to duplicate. This may well be the basis for some of the traditions surrounding magic done under specific moon phases. A subtle change in the mental state of a magician is often where an act of magic is manifested. This is the basis of all ritual. A ripple effect emanating from that subtle change can manifest into very solid results for the magician who understands the process.

Still, cold revenge you say... Let us consult the book of grudges 2:1-36...

- Diablo Verde

This leads us to the dangers of magic done in an unstable mental state. During anger, under the influence of too much alcohol, or during a particularly bad case of PMT is not time to attempt serious magic. You just might get what you wish for, and regret it for a long time. I have seen a woman with a bad case of post-partum depression throw random magic around her to the detriment of her own situation and everyone around her. It wasn't pretty. The woman who learns to recognise and balance her hormonal fluctuations might have fared better and used the disruption to more productive use.

Hell hath no fury...

There are many different aspects to attitudes of power and of female empowerment. I've always felt that the most vocal of the 1970's feminists took the wrong attitude, demanding equality with men and trying to imitate their mode of dress and habits. All we got out of it really was a higher level of high blood pressure and heart disease. There were some good things done by the movement, especially in areas of employment opportunities and rights, but in fighting for the material things, many of these women missed the opportunity to embrace much that is special and unique to the privilege of being a woman.

The primary purpose of this book is to explore ways in which a woman, or a man who works with one or more of them, might learn to embrace the strengths of feminine magic. Not feminist magic, but feminine magic. Women have referred to their menstrual cycle and all that goes with it by derogatory names including "the curse". Living with disruption and change does not suit everyone, yet it is thrust to some degree on every woman because of her inescapable biological nature.

But there is power in change, and in disruption. These are the precursors to new conditions, and what is magic for if not to create a change and bring about new conditions? This is why women are particularly suited to chaos magic or other freeform expressions of magic. The regimented Orders created by 19th century men have great value, but they were not created for the nature of the woman magician. To express her abilities fully, she will have to move beyond the traditions and practices which are taught through these Orders, into the uncharted territory of feminine magic.

Many female magicians have discovered this for themselves. Most of them have become the solitary magicians that I spoke of earlier in this book. Some have formed into working groups that are usually guided by pagan traditions. Very few have actually formed into small enclaves of women alchemists and magicians. It would be difficult to find many women on this path in any one area to form such a group.

A woman who discovers the power inherent in her changing hormonal cycles can be very formidable as a magician. Becoming attuned to these cycles so that the disruption of change becomes something to be embraced can be combined with her innate ability for enchantment, and then the magician is ready to move into a uniquely feminine form of sexual magic.

Summer is fast on it's way and I believe the mythos sap rises within us all...

- Diablo Verde

Chapter Eleven

Women and Sex Magic

The very mention of sex magic carries an element of fascination and intrigue for many people. I can easily predict that a large number of people who pick up this book from a shelf will turn to this chapter first, just out of curiosity to see what I have to say about it. In Western occultism, much of the association of sex with magic comes from the East, in translations of Tantra. Yet sex magic is also practised in more basic forms including sexual initiations and very basic power raising exercises that draw from the Tantric basis. Very little is said in most books about the power that sexuality itself provides for a woman.

Sex has a power behind it that taps into our most basic animal nature, and yet its real power far transcends the animal urge to rut. Techniques of sex magic use that primal force and direct its power to acts of very strong magic. Throughout human history, there have been regulations and taboos attached to sexuality, and espccially of a woman's place within sexual politics and control. Much of the controls that patriarchal society have historically put onto a woman's sexuality are obviously based in fear of man's own weakness against his own sexual attraction to the female, as is illustrated in the character of Frollo in the classic, *The Hunchback of Notre Dame*. It is Frollo's weakness for the allure of the gypsy Esmerelda that drives him to destroy her.

The very term 'sex magic' provokes a reaction from most people, especially those who are new to the term. Some immediately intellectualise the concept and think of higher techniques of Tantra and energy manipulation. Others imagine the completely uncontrolled force of sexuality in its most intimate moments and the potential of channelling such a force towards a desired magical goal. Both are equally important aspects of sexual magic.

In Western societies where women have reacted against repression of their sexuality with political movements for equality, there has been a loss of some of the more feminine aspects of her sexuality and therefore of an important element in her natural power. We could learn from the Eastern disciplines where the intimacy and deep connection shared by two people who share energy during magical sex forms a balance of power, which is truly lovemaking in its most glorious form.

Gnosis and altered states of mind can be achieved during the act of sex, even more so with intentional magical sex. Sexual gnosis is relatively easy to obtain, even without a partner, and is usable for charging spells in their most basic form. It is fairly well known that the magician Austin Osman Spare commonly charged his sigil spells through auto-eroticism. It is also known that his magic was incredibly effective.

In Tantra, sexuality is treated as a natural function of the body that must be kept balanced with as much care as nutrition and general physical well-being. Much of what one will read about Tantra will emphasise that balance must be achieved through sexuality, rather than the imbalances that over-concern about sex and the seedier side of eroticism may cause. Yet some of the Western practices used by some magicians today have delved into the world of sensory experimentation which can be achieved through acts of bondage, use of blindfolds, and other alternative sensory practises that might otherwise be looked upon with misunderstanding by a repressed society. These acts, used properly, can actually lead to deeply spiritual states of mind and body in union.

Being denied access to your senses and movement brings the consciousness into the body in a much fuller way... e.g. by being denied sight (with a blindfold) you are much more aware of sounds, sensations and energy. This focussed awareness is a powerful magical technique. Working with a partner within these disciplines requires a great deal of trust, yet many of them can be utilised while working alone. Restriction of movement does bring safety issues however, and is not recommended without the attendance of a well-trusted working partner. Like most things, it is worth becoming aware of the basic safety issues in advance. Experimental bondage can go wrong if the participants have not learned the techniques to allow proper circulation and quick escape methods (like keeping a pair of heavy duty scissors handy in case of emergencies).

Many old love spells make use of sexual fluids, specifically sperm or menstrual blood. The power of menstrual blood in magic has long been recognised, and was referred to by Aleister Crowley. Austin Spare of course consecrated his sigils with his own sperm. One of my old pet peeves in today's magical climate is the attempts to bring political correctness to Sparean methods by suggesting that the female magician obtain her own sexual fluids through sexual stimulation in some form, but this ignores the significance of the fertilising properties of the fluids. It is in fact more effective for a female magician to use menstrual blood in the magical formulae. It is this fluid which would feed the life in an act of fertilisation. The combined sexual fluids of male and female have a strong power used in unison, but those fluids which serve the purpose of lubrication alone lack the vital essence of the life-giving force which is employed in this form of magic.

Again, we come back to the act of sex for obtaining the required fluids which may be used in a sexual magic spell. Sexual stimulation does raise a great deal of magical energy, and properly channelled, this can be utilised in ritual. Because of its personal nature, this form of ritual is most often practised between partners, but not universally. Society has put many taboos on the practises of sexual intimacy, especially for women. Yet a woman magician who has liberated herself from these taboos can find a lot of scope for employing this form of energy to her rituals, whether it is raised by a relationship partner or a working partner trained to the task. Some may even work sexually with a close working group.

Some magicians will choose to invoke deity in some form during the act of sex, and ask for blessings or help with the purpose of the magic. If one takes on the belief of the specific deities, the feeding and/or worship of a god and goddess can develop a great rapport with them in ritual, and an invocation during the ritual will let a certain aspect of deity into your body/mind so that the deity gets to experience sex through your body.

In mythology, women who acknowledge their sexuality are too often depicted as harlots and mothers of demons. In Jewish folklore for example, in the texts of the Cabbalah, Lillith whom many of us have heard of as the first wife of Adam, was known by such titles as the Mother of Demons, the Woman of Harlotry, and the Convolute Serpent. Lillith was portrayed as the mother of all demons, which she gave birth to after stealing the semen of sleeping men who slept alone, and impregnated herself with it. She induced spontaneous emission in her lovers by causing them to experience erotic dreams. Notice the similarity to Frollo, who blames his own lust on the gypsy Esmerelda, who must be a witch to induce such reactions from himself.

Lillith is also associated by some sources with Naamah, who in the Bible was the sister of Tubalcain, "An instructor of every artificer in brass and iron." In the literature of the Kabalah, Naamah was transformed into a beautiful seductress who comes to the beds of men sleeping alone and makes love to them. At first she appears as the most beautiful woman imaginable. Again, the seductress is treated as a creature of deceit, who steals the semen of men for her own purposes. With Naamah the emphasis is on the sexual act and its pleasures. She is the beautiful Houri of forbidden lust, and embodies the enormous power of sexual energy to corrupt and seduce, as well as to give joy.

Lillith embodies the power of sexual energy to create and bring forth into manifest being, a power that can be perverted to create monsters. She is sexual energy used for creative purposes not sanctioned by the holy Torah. In Jewish folklore, all sexual pleasures that are enjoyed for their own sake fall under the command and control of Lillith, or her daughter Naamah, as all such unions are unlawful.

This mythology has many points in common with the stories of Tiamat, a Babylonian goddess who takes a serpentine form and begets monsters and demons. Serpent symbolism permeates many mythologies where sexual imagery plays a part. Yet if one looks beyond the associations with the evils of temptation that are placed on this symbolism, invariably there will be an older version of the religion which celebrates fertility, where Tiamat or many other goddesses will be the Great Mother rather than a begetter of demons. Sexuality is a powerful force that is largely in the control of the female of most species', and this power has been suppressed in patriarchal societies out of fear. By controlling the sexuality of the women, those creatures with the creative force inherent in their nature, the men of many cultures have maintained at least the illusion of control in their own societies. Still, the Primordial Force has a feminine nature.

Trickster figures, like many heroes in old tales, are most often male. But there are females among them as well. It is little remembered that Coyote sometimes encounters a female Coyote in some of the tales from the Hopi and Tewa Indians, both of which are matrilineal. Part of the reason for this may be that one of the attributes of trickster figures is lust, which many cultures do not like to credit to the female of the species. Like the mythologies of gods, lust is treated as a temptation to lure an unwitting victim into trouble of some sort.

Yet some of the old temples of India have carvings which depict sexual acts that would seem to have no place in a strongly patriarchal society. Holistic medicine, much of it based on treatments that come to us from Eastern cultures, acknowledges the need for a healthy sex life in achieving overall balance of the body. Sex is known to relieve stress. Cultural conditioning may require that sexuality is practised within committed relationships in many cultures, but sexuality itself is undeniably healthy and a strong requirement of our most basic physical health.

In magic, the physical balance that is attained through a healthy sex life will reflect in the magician's overall spiritual balance, and the creative principles reflected in acts of sex can be put to magical use. After all, what is magic but a creative act?

Not all acts of sexual magic have to require copulation. Magical tradition embraces many symbolic acts that may be used in group rituals where some form of sexuality may be depicted without falling into a raging orgy. The well-known 'Great Rite' of Wicca tradition for example, where an Athame is plunged symbolically into a Chalice in representation of the sexual act, is fairly commonly practised in public ceremonies that are suited even for children to witness. While an act that has removed the tradition so far from its more literal roots may seem stale to magicians who practise more erotic magic, it serves a purpose for the public face of the magical community without challenging the inhibitions of onlookers or the cultural conditioning of the participants too far.

Sexuality is inherently practised in Dance magic. Rhythmic and enticing movements of the body are one of the oldest forms of magic known to humankind. Dance is sensuality, and is inherently suggestive. It is practised in some form among many animals, especially bird species' who often have mating dances to attract partners. The popularity of bellydancing, a form of dance that is undeniably enticing, among modern pagan communities is at least at a subconscious level, an acknowledgement of the connection between magic and sensuality.

Some forms of sex magic can be practised indirectly, such as seed sigils. A plant seed of some sort is either gently carved with a sigil, or named with one if it is too small for carving. The seed is planted in the course of a ritual charging, and then cared for daily much like a progression spell. The creation of new life is a powerful form of magic.

Fear of sexuality has repressed much of the natural magic in women magicians for centuries. A woman who takes conscious control of her sexuality and recognises the inherent power within is in a position to employ this potent resource to her magic. She does not have to compromise her personal morals or become promiscuous to do this, but can work within the confines of a relationship if she chooses, or select suitable working partners according to her own criteria. Taking control of choice is part of the power. And in fact, such power of choice has been a factor for centuries in many very, very old forms of magic.

Hmmm...
You know what you're talking about...
this could be a tough one...

- Diablo Verde

Chapter Twelve

Old Magic In A New Age

In today's world where New Age subjects have become mainstream and even your manager at work might happily admit to having an interest in crystal therapy or past life regression memories, it is easy to forget that just a few decades ago, these were taboo subjects, spoken of only by a few weirdlings and the occasional friend's maiden aunt. It is easy to lose sight of where much of today's superstition and pop culture magical merchandising draws from the very real magic that is as old as time itself. Conversely, the tendency to try to attribute old roots to some of the modern methods becomes almost comical in its sincerity and delusion.

Yet behind the commercial façade which has become the public face of magic in the new age, there is a very basic need within the human spirit to have some sort of connection to an aspect of the spiritual. Many people are fascinated by the archaic, and the spiritual aspects of ancient cultures. The Egyptians for example, with their devotion to pure spiritual power as well as to tremendous monuments; the Greeks and their great philosophical writings; and even to scientific discoveries which carry a form of spiritual belief of their own.

At the basis of science was once Alchemy, which sought to refine arts that are now thought of as impossible. Yet there is some evidence that a very few might have reached success in their quest for the Philosopher's Stone.

'Magic' is often the science that mankind hasn't learned to explain yet. However, some things never will be explained or repeatable in laboratories. Scientists periodically convince themselves (and many of us) that they have the power to explain everything in the physical world. The belief system asserts that everything is reducible to particles and waves at a quantum level, or beyond. The trouble is that every time the scientific community begins to believe that they've got all the details of life, the universe and everything worked out, something unexpected happens.

Many of the discoveries of science have served to explain aspects of magic. Alchemy becomes chemistry, chaos theory explains probability, and everything comes down to what is considered the last frontier, the human mind. A fair few scientists even believe that they understand that, but I have watched various people pigeonholed into neat little textbook boxes of psychiatric classification that didn't quite fit the evidence of independent thought and perception. The tendency of the modern psychiatric world is to drug those who deviate from these boxes and invent childhood 'disorders' like ODD (Oppositional Defiance Disorder, i.e. a child who doesn't do what they are told to). After seeing the damage done to people by misclassification and inappropriate drug therapy, I cannot help but to perceive the most smug of psychiatrists with their Ph.D.'s proudly displayed behind their desks as egotistical children, convinced that they know everything there is to know while the obvious flies past them.

Let me state here that I have never been under psychiatric care of any kind myself and do not hold any personal resentments to the profession, and I happily agree that there are practitioners within it who are very helpful to their clients and able to administer appropriate drugs or other therapies. These will be the more open-minded individuals who have the wisdom and courage to admit that they don't always know everything after a half-hour session with a new client. But I have seen people close to me suffer from the administrations of those who believe too fully in their own infallibility.

Magicians and scientists have more in common than either is likely to want to admit. Both are subject to the belief that they have answers that others do not, and to the arrogance that actually having some of these answers can bring. It is fairly well-known that I am a chaos magician. Chaos is an area where magic and science can overlap, and is therefore subject to the insolence of belief that one really does understand the workings of the universe more than either of the other two camps.

One of the attributes of chaos magic is simplicity of method, or short-cuts if you will. This is where a lot of new magicians who go straight into chaos magic without a basis in any of the old magics can lose out. They get into short-cut magical methods without learning the basics behind them and then complain when their magic doesn't work, and ask the 'experienced' magicians to hand it to them on a plate as if it could be bottled and sold. They want to believe that magic is real and may have some minor successes to spur them on, but significant change will elude them and so they spend their time on internet forums asking advice rather than applying themselves to serious study.

I have been questioned before about why I recommend that new magicians work on a magical path other than chaos before beginning to use chaos magic. It is because I've observed that people who go directly into chaos magic often miss much basic information. Chaos magic was started by experienced magicians and is often geared towards them.

With time the training programmes may become more effective, but on chaos e-mail lists you will see a lot of people complaining that their magic isn't working. This is because they haven't learned the 'feel' of magic before going into short-cut techniques. However well they understand the theory, they've missed something.

I have a friend who is a successful chaos magician, who started his magical practice in chaos. He has impressed me by putting himself on a programme to learn magic the old fashioned way, with the complete formal ritual that old traditions require. These are very valuable lessons. Chaos magic comes with a lot of psychobabble and standard theories and such, but what it is missing is a touchy-feely approach that makes all the difference in successful magic. Many of the elements of ritual which are steeped in tradition serve to bring the magician into a mental state where magic becomes possible. Modern methods bypass much of this, and while they certainly eliminate the superstition and fear that has accompanied magic in the past, they also miss out on the spiritual aspects of magic. This is the same mistake that so many of the European alchemists made.

If you could use Kirlian photography to record the changes in a magician in deep ritual, you would find that Spirit is not just a matter of superstition, but a measurable quantity that can be observed as an energy field. It can effect changes in the area around the magician, and if magical theory is to be believed, this can have far reaching effects far away from the magician's physical presence. In chaos science, a theory to support this is demonstrated by the Butterfly Effect. It is ironic that if you used the same Kirlian photography to record the Auric field of some of the more empirical modern magicians, it would be easy to see that the build-up of this energy field is much less of a factor in their magical methods, and thus in the results. This is one area where the female magician has an advantage in that her naturally emotional approach to magic is more conducive to such energy build-up than her more scientific-minded counterpart.

The role of emotion and subjective perception play an essential role in magic. The ability to sense when something is working smoothly or when something feels wrong is needed in order to adequately supervise and influence the progression of a magical act, just as the senses of a mother hearing her child come in will tell her of the child's mood from another room. The role of the feminine element, water, in alchemical symbolism is paradoxical in that it holds an equal position with the other elements, yet despite its natural mutability in action, it is the symbol which holds the most stability in representation. The balance of the four basic elements is represented by the four armed cross.

In alchemical symbolism, the four-armed cross plays an important role, yet is never found in isolation, but combined with other symbols to create a deeper meaning. It is interesting to note that one of these symbols is commonly used to refer to the female, and also to the planet Venus. The circle which comprises the other part of this symbol is also highly significant. While the cross symbolises the balance of the elemental forces, the circle represents the beginning and ending of all things, the circle of life, the cycles of birth and death, the first matter, Ouroboros, the culmination of all. It is that which encloses all, and yet is the all within. The circle features in the symbols for both male and female, but for the male we add the arrow of progression while for the female, we have the cross of balance. Both are necessary qualities in an act of alchemical magic.

The concept of the four elements, Earth, Air, Fire and Water, originally comes to us from alchemy. It was actually Paracelsus who first referred to the elemental spirits as Gnomes, Sylphs, Undines and Salamanders which are in common use among Wiccans today. The symbolism has

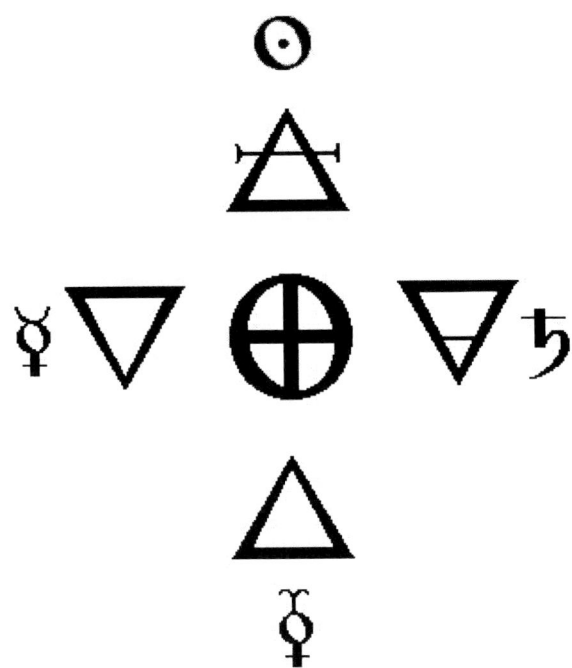

adapted over time as symbolism will, and various belief systems have changed the positions for the elements. This is not really important in the systems of magic where it has occurred, as the positions serve only as symbols within those disciplines.

In most modern Wicca groups, you will learn that Earth is North, Fire South, Air to the East, Water to the West. This system is actually based in Middle Eastern religion. Some old British traditional groups place the Earth South (below), Air North (above), Fire to the East (where the Sun rises) and Water to the West (the vast ocean). There is a logic to this; you stand on the Earth, the Air is above you, the Fire of the Sun rises in the east and the vast Ocean is to the west. This is the symbolism I have used in the Centre of Chaos banishing which is published in *Chaos Monkey* (Capall Bann, 2003) and on various websites.

The alchemical symbolism from whence these others arise places Fire below, Earth above, Air to the right and Water to the left. Yet a traditional alchemical diagram shows still another arrangement, with Air above, Fire below, Earth to the right and Water to the left. It is interesting to note that the only one of these elements that stays consistent in position is Water. Water plays a very significant role in alchemy, although not always strictly as itself. The mercurial waters spoken of in some old alchemical texts are fluids of a more toxic kind, yet retain mysteries of transmutation that are essential to the understanding of the alchemical arts.

The serious study of alchemy and other old magics can be laborious, yet rewarding. The female magician who has always thought of the dusty old tomes as a man's world may be surprised to learn how many women have studied these arts through history, and at how well the methods suit her natural disposition. She may even see wisdom between the lines that were written from a male perspective in another age, when women were generally not thought of as potential alchemists and magicians. Some of the writers of the tomes themselves might be surprised to learn what Flamel knew, that in fact it was the disposition of a woman that was missing from their ancient formulae, and that it might have even been this that could have been the key to their eventual success.

*I look forward to seeing what becomes of you. I suspect I've a
bit of Serpent in me, I just hope no one lets David Icke know,
he'll be round here with his scalpel and camcorder...*
- Diablo Verde

Chapter Thirteen

Coming Into Her Own

One of the most intimidating figures in Western society is
that of the Matriarch, the woman who has lived long enough
to gain experience and who recognises the importance of her
place in a family unit. This is the sort of woman who wields
authority not by demand, but by expectation of respect. There
is a particular calm form of power that comes from surviving
everything life can throw at you and sorting out the problems
of those around you along the way as well. A woman need not
have power over a family or clan to reach this sort of self-
assurance, but only over herself and her own life.

The woman who learns to understand the use of magic in her
own terms may well reach this level of capability long before
she is of an age to become a family elder. It is those women
among the magicians who exude the sort of confidence that
indicates that she can cope with anything that needs sorting
whom the patriarchal-minded males find most intimidating.
She makes it clear that she doesn't need a man to survive,
even though she may choose to share her life with one because
she enjoys his companionship. She becomes respected because
she always has an answer for any problem or difficult

situation. She simply looks at the options and suggests the best possible choice.

Women have been associated with mystery in various cultures for centuries, and that is what can inspire fear, even from men in very male dominated societies. They look for logic and control where there is emotion and resilience, and beneath it all is a form of awe for the woman's ability to produce new life, however much a man may take credit for seeding it. Women are the unknown, and mysterious like cats. Just when they think they have us worked out, we do something unex-pected. Not because we make a conscious decision to be unpredictable, but because we simply think differently and sometimes in the abstract. A man will seek to solve a problem with linear thought and logic, while the woman will take in the subtle and far reaching influences on the situation and come to a conclusion that only that elusive thing called intuition could reach.

We also have the ability to stand up under ridiculous amounts of pressure and can often be the one keeping a cool head in a crisis. Women have been the strength behind successful men as well as the matriarchal figure that leads with unfailing resolve. Although most often not as physically strong as our male companions, it is the women who maintain inner strength in times of greatest challenge. This can be daunting to some.

In many mythologies, the tree is representative of the great cosmic mother in various forms, or the Divine Mother. We see tree associations with Istar, Anat, Tammuz, Cybele. In the Edda it is the goddess Idhunn who is charged with guarding the apples of immortality. There are obvious fertility associations with this tree association, but also associations with oracles and knowledge. The 'women's intuition' we spoke of earlier may be associated with her procreative principles, but it can also be employed in the greater spectrum of magical practice and knowledge.

A woman magician interprets magical theory differently than her male counterpart. Her natural affinity with the creative principle makes her a natural practitioner of the Arts of sorcery, despite centuries of superstitions and taboos which have restricted women in many cultures from fully exploring the knowledge and practise of magic. Chaos magic in particular suits her disposition, even though it was labelled and categorised by male magicians. There were magicians who did not hesitate to work with women, or to explore the feminine principles in magic.

Without the balance of masculine and feminine, yin and yang, nothing in nature is complete. Magic is a part of the natural world, and the suppression, neglect or separation of the feminine side of it has limited the full potential and expression of magic in the western world for far too long. The male magicians of the past few centuries have left great legacies of information and technique, but it is time that the woman magician recognised that like a recipe, these are guidelines rather than hard and fast rules. The books are writings of other magicians; a source for information which must then be adapted for the perspective of the new magicians who are meant to learn from them.

The time for a separation of male techniques in ceremonial magic to be separated from the feminine principle in modern witchcraft is past. While these disciplines will no doubt continue in their current forms for some time to come, the women magicians who bring their feminine perspective to the world of magic(k) are more plentiful than many of them realise, and a conscious recognition of the value of their approach to magic is long overdue. At least among ourselves.

Whether we choose to work alone, with a group, or with a trusted partner, it is time the female magician became fully aware that our approach to magic can and must be as different to that of the men who wrote the books as it is different to our approach to everything else in life from the men we choose to share ours with. It is not a matter of being 'better', but of recognising that we are different because we are women, and can blossom into our full potential best by utilising the qualities that come natural to us as women. Women of power.

JAQ!! YOU MUST BE ENTRUSTED THIS MOST HOLY TASK! NOTE DOWN AND KEEP RECORDED IN A NON ELECTRONIC FORM THE PHRASES THAT ARE UTTERED FROM MINE HOLIEST OF MOUTHS AND KEEPING THEREIN THE WORDS OF WISDOM AND HILARITY THAT ARE UTTERED!!! SO IT IS WRITTEN!!! SO LET IT BE DONE!!!! Ahem.

- Diablo Verde

Appendix

Progression Sigils
(Reprinted from Chaos International
Volumes 24 & 25)

Note: Sigils are only one form of magic that lends itself well to progression spells. Any spell which is performed over a period of time to build up energy can be extremely powerful. This reprinted article (slightly adapted for book inclusion) is one example of an effective method which has been successfully used by the author.

Part 1

A progression sigil is a magical technique wherein several sigils may be used to represent sequential or complex aspects of an intent. I have worked with progression spells in various forms for many years, but this sigil technique was actually given to me as a gift from an Occultist in the 1980's, and was immediately adapted to my own use.

The basic technique as given to me follows a sequence. Five sigils are drawn in the usual way. They are laid out in the ritual space in preparation for charging, using directional symbolism as suits the magician. The first sigil represents the magician him/herself, and the second represents the situation which is relevant to the magic being performed. These two sigils fill the top two positions of the inverted Pentagram, as in Figure 1. The other three sigils represent the progressions which the magician wishes to see manifest in relation to the situation. These are laid out in their appropriate positions, and given the appropriate charge.

Figure 1

A variation of this works with simultaneous aspects of the intent, still using the 'self' for the starting point but using elemental representations to coincide with chosen deities. Notice that in both cases, the charge is to be performed moving clockwise (Deosil) around the Pentagram rather than Widdershins. This is because creative energy works in a clockwise direction in the Northern hemisphere, and the spell is likely to involve creating a result. In my own method which will be more fully explained in part 2 of this article, Widdershins sigils can be used for purposes which would normally be associated with waning Moon activities, such as removing something from your life.

For the sake of simplicity I will picture the associations with a 'point-up' Pentagram in Figure 2. The uppermost point is to represent the magician, and the call will be his or her own magical name. One might notice that the order of the elements differs from the popular Wiccan associations. The names of each of the deities will be called in turn, as the magician turns clockwise around the magical space and points the wand at each of the points of the Pentagram. It is important that the associations of the deities to the element are uppermost in the mind rather than the specifics of the sigil which has been drawn to represent each of the aspects. The same charging is used for both methods discussed so far, the only difference being a subtle one in that method one progresses a series of actions to manifest while method two focuses on elemental associations, i.e. the emotional issues in the Water sigil, actions to occur in Fire, intellectual aspects in Air and solid, material matters in Earth.

Figure 2

This charging can be incorporated into any form of ritual. Details of these I will leave to the individual, as there are differences between groups as to how they choose to perform these rituals.

My own variation of this method takes the entire process into a written form, to be treated much like any other sigil. Rather than placing sigils in geographical locations in the ritual space, they are represented on parchment as a combined sigil as in Figure 3.

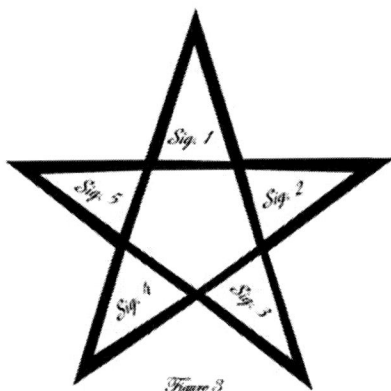

This method uses similar representations for aspects relating to the intent, but because I do not work with a specific pantheon, I have completely left out deity as well as the elemental associations and applied this to my own progression methods. These include using position 1 to represent the main focus of the intent, and following the progressions or variable aspects around the circle of the Pentagram accordingly. In some cases, the central intent may well fill the centre of the Pentagram itself with yet another combined sigil, possibly made up of the design of the other 5 designs. The Pentagram itself is drawn on a circle cut from parchment paper, so that the points reach to the edge of the paper. The diameter of a Campbell's soup tin I find is ideal size for this circle of parchment.

Part 2

In the first part of this article, I explained the basic concept of Progression Sigils and drew several examples of how they might be laid out. What I didn't mention was that the original charging formula, as dramatic as it may sound, is something I've never personally used. The names of deities simply do not strike a chord with my personal use of symbolism in magic.

As a Chaos Magician, I found it only natural to adapt the original formula from my very first experiments with it to methods which I could find more meaningful. Oddly enough, the one thing I did not adapt is the original Pentagram diagram. It would be a temptation for any Chaos Magician to apply this formula to an eight-pointed star design, and I may well try it some day if a purpose occurs where that much detail seems appropriate, but so far to date I have found that breaking a purpose down into five (a significant Discordian number anyway) stages is just about right for an actual working.

Any number of progressions is, of course, possible. One might use any geometric design one chooses to symbolise the workings of a progression spell, although something as complicated as John Dee's Sigillum Dei AEmeth may be too complicated when it comes to focusing on the order of the progression. A simple Pentagram with five sequential sigils placed in the points of the star, following a straight forward progression either deosil or widdershins depending on the intent and the choice of the magician, keeps it basic. The effectiveness of such basic methods is well known among most experienced magicians.

Those who are familiar with the methods of Austin Osman Spare will immediately see the value of using bodily fluids in charging spells for this sort of sigil. I have found this to be a very natural and effective ingredient in whatever spell I have worked with this method. Using either combined male and female sexual fluids or menstrual blood to 'consecrate' the sigil a day before the actual drawing of the individual progression sigils allows the spell to begin the feeling of time continuum, as well as allowing the fluids to dry for practical purposes. Then the actual designs can be added during the chosen ritual itself, and sealed in afterwards with more fluids of a chosen type either at the end of the ritual or at a later time.

Another aspect of this sort of spell which I find appropriate is to concoct a simple daily ritual dedicated to its purpose, and to utilise the finished sigil in its daily performance over a period of time. I have done such chargings over as little as a week, and in one serious case for three months. The results were astounding in both cases, but the longer time period, combined with a period of fasting (in this case fasting from all sugar, not an easy choice for a chocoholic), was enough to turn a major foreign judicial system on its head. Performing a daily ritual in pretty much the same sequence every day is an essential aspect in progression rituals. A simple ritual is best. The daily performance becomes boring, but that is exactly the point. Over a long enough period of time, the actions required become ingrained into the consciousness of the magician in the way of any daily habit, and subsequently charge the sigil perhaps even more exhaustively than a sigil which has been charged through the more abrupt forms of charging such as orgasm. Also, the daily habits are such a relief to abandon when the time period is finished that the release of the daily ritual acts as a release for the magic as well.

Progression spells are something which I would not advise using for everyday magical requirements. Like any method, they can become stale with over-use. However, they are probably the most effective method I have encountered for extremely important purposes, especially those with a low probability factor. It is important for each element of the sigil that much thought is put into exactly what is desired. The old adage, "Be careful what you wish for", is multiplied by the number of individual sigils applied in this method. The order of the progression is also worth a clear evaluation before beginning. The possibilities for this method to become unstable and chaotic are far greater than in any single purpose spell, and the magician must be prepared to redirect any aspect of the spell which becomes imbalanced. The daily ritual of charging is the appropriate time and place to assess and gently nudge (in butterfly fashion) the physical progression of the spell, up until the time period for the daily chargings expires. After that, it's too late. Extra thought put into the closing of the final ritual to 'seal' the spell's direction is highly recommended.

Of course, more gentle progression spells can be achieved by using a daily ritual for a specified period of time omitting the sigil completely. This method creates gentle waves of magic over a period of time rather than concentrating the energy into a physical representation to be destroyed at the end, thereby releasing the accumulated force of magic with all the impact of a magical bomb.

The daily charging method can be almost ecclesiastical in its simplicity, performed over a candle or two, in appearances not much different than a basic Wiccan ritual or Catholic prayer. The difference, as in most Chaos Magic operations, is in attitude and approach. The daily ritual is approached with intent rather than reverence or unformed desire. The will is focused on a specific change, a result. The performance of the ritual itself does not come from a meaningless prescribed formula, but is individually chosen by the magician according to the symbols and methods most relevant to the individual.

What connects this ritual method to the progression sigil method laid out in part 1 of this article is the build up of magical power as well as the inclusion of several elements.

The ritual may follow a sequence of events as described in fig. 1 of part 1, or several simultaneous changes required as explained in fig. 2. Those who wish to try the original charging formula are welcome to do so, and I would very much like to hear of any results, but take no responsibility for anything which may go wrong. The originators of the method themselves believe in self-responsibility, and those who use these methods are accountable to themselves.

The most effective magic works on chaotic principles, and a spell method with potentially chaotic possibilities is most often the key to succeeding in low probability cases. The progression sigil is probably the most chaotic method I know, and yet it is also the method wherein correcting imbalances which affect the spell is most possible. My first serious attempt with this method was thrown way out of balance when a divorce was thrown at me in a feeble attempt to pull me out of the magical paradigm for the sake of an attention seeker, who was soon after completely eliminated from my life, and re-balancing the ritual in progress required complete focus on the intent to the absolute exclusion of the distraction.

That is the one potential difficulty of this form of ritual, one is never completely out of ritual during the time period of the progressive charging. It becomes necessary to go about your daily activities in an almost zombie fashion, part of the mind continually focused on the ritual in progress. Distractions must be shut out, as every perception or action surrounding the life of the magician during that time carries a risk of effecting the ritual at hand. I advise against reading fiction at all during such times.

This capacity for aberration in the magic is part of what makes it so potent. The necessity of keeping focus throughout the appearance of mundane existence is no easy task even for the most seasoned of magicians. The possibility that a stray thought may send the direction of the spell into an unintentional direction is a constant danger, and yet the excitement of such danger is part of the gnosis which makes the method so powerful. This is truly the art of living on the edge of Chaos.

Bibliography and Recommended Reading

Ashanti, Dr. Kwabena F. *Rootwork and Voodoo in Mental Health*, Durham, NC: Tone Books,1987.

Dukes, Ramsey. *The Good, the Bad, the Funny*. London: The Mouse That Spins, 2002.

Evola, Julius. *The Hermetic Tradition*. Rochester, Vermont: Inner Traditions, 1971.

Lai, Hsi. *The Sexual Teachings of the White Tigress*. Rochester, VT: Destiny Books, 2001.

Mace, Stephen. *Addressing Power*. Self-Published, 1996.

Marshall, Peter. *The Philosopher's Stone: A Quest for the Secrets of Alchemy*. London: Pan Books, 2001.

Mate, Mavis E. *Women in Medieval English Society*. Cambridge: Cambridge University Press, 1999.

Nema. *Maat Magick*. York Beach, ME: Samuel Weiser, 1995.

Skelton, Robin. *Spellcraft*. London and Henley: Routledge & Kegan Paul, 1978.

Tyson, Donald. *Sexual Alchemy; Magical Intercourse with Spirits*. Woodbury, MN: Llewellyn, 2000.

Watterson, Barbara. *Women in Ancient Egypt*. Gloucester: Alan Sutton Publishing Ltd, 1991.

West, Kate. *The Real Witches Kitchen*. Pittsburgh: HarperCollins, 2002.

Internet Sources:
http://www.healthyplace.com/communities/depression/related/suicide_8.asp

http://www.siu.edu/~ebl/leaflets/greentea.htm

Index

FREE DETAILED CATALOGUE

Capall Bann is owned and run by people actively involved in many of the areas in which we publish. A detailed illustrated catalogue is available on request, SAE or International Postal Coupon appreciated. **Titles can be ordered direct from Capall Bann, post free in the UK** (cheque or PO with order) or from good bookshops and specialist outlets.

A Breath Behind Time, Terri Hector
A Soul is Born by Eleyna Williamson
Angels and Goddesses - Celtic Christianity & Paganism, M. Howard
The Art of Conversation With the Genius Loci, Barry Patterson
Arthur - The Legend Unveiled, C Johnson & E Lung
Astrology The Inner Eye - A Guide in Everyday Language, E Smith
Auguries and Omens - The Magical Lore of Birds, Yvonne Aburrow
Asyniur - Womens Mysteries in the Northern Tradition, S McGrath
Beginnings - Geomancy, Builder's Rites & Electional Astrology in the
    European Tradition, Nigel Pennick
Between Earth and Sky, Julia Day
Book of the Veil , Peter Paddon
The Book of Seidr, Runic John
Caer Sidhe - Celtic Astrology and Astronomy, Michael Bayley
Call of the Horned Piper, Nigel Jackson
Can't Sleep, Won't Sleep, Linga Louisa Dell
Carnival of the Animals, Gregor Lamb
Cat's Company, Ann Walker
Celtic Faery Shamanism, Catrin James
Celtic Faery Shamanism - The Wisdom of the Otherworld, Catrin James
Celtic Lore & Druidic Ritual, Rhiannon Ryall
Celtic Sacrifice - Pre Christian Ritual & Religion, Marion Pearce
Celtic Saints and the Glastonbury Zodiac, Mary Caine
Circle and the Square, Jack Gale
Come Back To Life, Jenny Smedley
Compleat Vampyre - The Vampyre Shaman, Nigel Jackson
Creating Form From the Mist - The Wisdom of Women in Celtic Myth and
    Culture, Lynne Sinclair-Wood
Crystal Clear - A Guide to Quartz Crystal, Jennifer Dent
Crystal Doorways, Simon & Sue Lilly
Crossing the Borderlines - Guising, Masking & Ritual Animal Disguise in the
    European Tradition, Nigel Pennick

Dragons of the West, Nigel Pennick
Earth Dance - A Year of Pagan Rituals, Jan Brodie
Earth Harmony - Places of Power, Holiness & Healing, Nigel Pennick
Earth Magic, Margaret McArthur
Egyptian Animals - Guardians & Gateways of the Gods, Akkadia Ford
Eildon Tree (The) Romany Language & Lore, Michael Hoadley
Enchanted Forest - The Magical Lore of Trees, Yvonne Aburrow
Eternal Priestess, Sage Weston
Eternally Yours Faithfully, Roy Radford & Evelyn Gregory
Everything You Always Wanted To Know About Your Body, But So Far
    Nobody's Been Able To Tell You, Chris Thomas & D Baker
Experiencing the Green Man, Rob Hardy & Teresa Moorey
Face of the Deep - Healing Body & Soul, Penny Allen
Fairies and Nature Spirits, Teresa Moorey
Fairies in the Irish Tradition, Molly Gowen
Familiars - Animal Powers of Britain, Anna Franklin
Flower Wisdom, Katherine Kear
Fool's First Steps, (The) Chris Thomas
Forest Paths - Tree Divination, Brian Harrison, Ill. S. Rouse
From Past to Future Life, Dr Roger Webber
Gardening For Wildlife Ron Wilson
God Year, The, Nigel Pennick & Helen Field
Goddess on the Cross, Dr George Young
Goddess Year, The, Nigel Pennick & Helen Field
Goddesses, Guardians & Groves, Jack Gale
Handbook For Pagan Healers, Liz Joan
Handbook of Fairies, Ronan Coghlan
Healing Book, The, Chris Thomas and Diane Baker
Healing Homes, Jennifer Dent
Healing Journeys, Paul Williamson
Healing Stones, Sue Philips
Herb Craft - Shamanic & Ritual Use of Herbs, Lavender & Franklin
Hidden Heritage - Exploring Ancient Essex, Terry Johnson
Hub of the Wheel, Skytoucher
In and Out the Windows, Dilys Gator
In Search of Herne the Hunter, Eric Fitch
In Search of the Green Man, Peter Hill
Inner Celtia, Alan Richardson & David Annwn
Inner Mysteries of the Goths, Nigel Pennick
Inner Space Workbook - Develop Thru Tarot, C Summers & J Vayne
Intuitive Journey, Ann Walker Isis - African Queen, Akkadia Ford
Journey Home, The, Chris Thomas
Kecks, Keddles & Kesh - Celtic Lang & The Cog Almanac, Bayley
Language of the Psycards, Berenice
Legend of Robin Hood, The, Richard Rutherford-Moore
Lid Off the Cauldron, Patricia Crowther

Light From the Shadows - Modern Traditional Witchcraft, Gwyn
Living Tarot, Ann Walker
Lore of the Sacred Horse, Marion Davies
Lost Lands & Sunken Cities (2nd ed.), Nigel Pennick
Magic For the Next 1,000 Years, Jack Gale
Magic of Herbs - A Complete Home Herbal, Rhiannon Ryall
Magical Guardians - Exploring the Spirit and Nature of Trees, Philip Heselton
Magical History of the Horse, Janet Farrar & Virginia Russell
Magical Lore of Animals, Yvonne Aburrow
Magical Lore of Cats, Marion Davies
Magical Lore of Herbs, Marion Davies
Magick Without Peers, Ariadne Rainbird & David Rankine
Masks of Misrule - Horned God & His Cult in Europe, Nigel Jackson
Medicine For The Coming Age, Lisa Sand MD
Medium Rare - Reminiscences of a Clairvoyant, Muriel Renard
Menopausal Woman on the Run, Jaki da Costa
Mind Massage - 60 Creative Visualisations, Marlene Maundrill
Mirrors of Magic - Evoking the Spirit of the Dewponds, P Heselton
The Moon and You, Teresa Moorey
Moon Mysteries, Jan Brodie
Mysteries of the Runes, Michael Howard
Mystic Life of Animals, Ann Walker
New Celtic Oracle The, Nigel Pennick & Nigel Jackson
Oracle of Geomancy, Nigel Pennick
Pagan Feasts - Seasonal Food for the 8 Festivals, Franklin & Phillips
Patchwork of Magic - Living in a Pagan World, Julia Day
Pathworking - A Practical Book of Guided Meditations, Pete Jennings
Personal Power, Anna Franklin
Pickingill Papers - The Origins of Gardnerian Wicca, Bill Liddell
Pillars of Tubal Cain, Nigel Jackson
Places of Pilgrimage and Healing, Adrian Cooper
Planet Earth - The Universe's Experiment, Chris Thomas
Practical Divining, Richard Foord
Practical Meditation, Steve Hounsome
Practical Spirituality, Steve Hounsome
Psychic Self Defence - Real Solutions, Jan Brodie
Real Fairies, David Tame
Reality - How It Works & Why It Mostly Doesn't, Rik Dent
Romany Tapestry, Michael Houghton
Runic Astrology, Nigel Pennick
Sacred Animals, Gordon MacLellan
Sacred Celtic Animals, Marion Davies, Ill. Simon Rouse
Sacred Dorset - On the Path of the Dragon, Peter Knight
Sacred Grove - The Mysteries of the Forest, Yvonne Aburrow
Sacred Geometry, Nigel Pennick
Sacred Nature, Ancient Wisdom & Modern Meanings, A Cooper

Sacred Ring - Pagan Origins of British Folk Festivals, M. Howard
Season of Sorcery - On Becoming a Wisewoman, Poppy Palin
Seasonal Magic - Diary of a Village Witch, Paddy Slade
Secret Places of the Goddess, Philip Heselton
Secret Signs & Sigils, Nigel Pennick
The Secrets of East Anglian Magic, Nigel Pennick
A Seeker's Guide To Past Lives, Paul Williamson
Seeking Pagan Gods, Teresa Moorey
A Seer's Guide To Crystal Divination, Gale Halloran
Self Enlightenment, Mayan O'Brien
Spirits of the Air, Jaq D Hawkins
Spirits of the Water, Jaq D Hawkins
Spirits of the Fire, Jaq D Hawkins
Spirits of the Aether, Jaq D Hawkins
Spirits of the Earth, Jaq D Hawkins
Stony Gaze, Investigating Celtic Heads John Billingsley
Stumbling Through the Undergrowth , Mark Kirwan-Heyhoe
Subterranean Kingdom, The, revised 2nd ed, Nigel Pennick
Symbols of Ancient Gods, Rhiannon Ryall
Talking to the Earth, Gordon MacLellan
Talking With Nature, Julie Hood
Taming the Wolf - Full Moon Meditations, Steve Hounsome
Teachings of the Wisewomen, Rhiannon Ryall
The Other Kingdoms Speak, Helena Hawley
Transformation of Housework, Ben Bushill
Tree: Essence of Healing, Simon & Sue Lilly
Tree: Essence, Spirit & Teacher, Simon & Sue Lilly
Tree Seer, Simon & Sue Lilly
Through the Veil, Peter Paddon
Torch and the Spear, Patrick Regan
Understanding Chaos Magic, Jaq D Hawkins
Understanding Past Lives, Dilys Gater
Understanding Second Sight, Dilys Gater
Understanding Spirit Guides, Dilys Gater
Understanding Star Children, **NEW** Dilys Gater
The Urban Shaman, Dilys Gater
Vortex - The End of History, Mary Russell
Warp and Weft - In Search of the I-Ching, William de Fancourt
Warriors at the Edge of Time, Jan Fry
Water Witches, Tony Steele
Way of the Magus, Michael Howard
Weaving a Web of Magic, Rhiannon Ryall
West Country Wicca, Rhiannon Ryall
What's Your Poison? vol 1, Tina Tarrant
Wheel of the Year, Teresa Moorey & Jane Brideson
Wildwitch - The Craft of the Natural Psychic, Poppy Palin

Wildwood King , Philip Kane
A Wisewoman's Book of Tea Leaf Reading, Pat Barki
The Witching Craft, Moira Stirland
The Witch's Kitchen, Val Thomas
Witches of Oz, Matthew & Julia Philips
Wondrous Land - The Faery Faith of Ireland by Dr Kay Mullin
Working With Crystals, Shirley o'Donoghue
Working With Natural Energy, Shirley o'Donoghue
Working With the Merlin, Geoff Hughes
Your Talking Pet, Ann Walker

FREE detailed catalogue and FREE 'Inspiration' magazine

Contact: Capall Bann Publishing, Auton Farm, Milverton, Somerset, TA4 1NE